DNA Activation

Using Multidimensional Sound & Music to Awaken Humanity's Highest Potentials

Also by Shapeshifter/Gary & JoAnn Chambers

Books

The Secret of Abundance: ReJuva

CD Soundscapes

DNA Activation LevelOne
DNA 1.5 Lucidity
DNA.L2.2012
Journey of the Soul
Abundance Series: ReJuva
Abundance Series: Sanctuary
Shamballa ~ Journey Home
TLC | Journey towards Ascension
11:11 Transmissions of Light Codes
Odyssey
Healing
Touch of Angels
Myth, Magic & Mystery

DVDs

Activate Your DNA
Shamanic Journeys into the Multidimensional Timestreams
AYD #1 - Building a Spiritual Foundation
AYD #2 - Working with Multidimensional Sound

All above titles available at VisionaryMusic.com
(music available on CD or as downloads)

Websites
VisionaryMusic.com
VisionaryMusic.net
ShapeshifterBlog.com
ActivateYourDNA.com
TransmissionsOfLightCodes.com
3rdEyeGuidance.com

Visit on MySpace, Facebook, Twitter, YouTube, Itunes Podcasts

DNA Activation

Using Multidimensional Sound & Music to Awaken Humanity's Highest Potentials

**Transmissions & Downloads
Received by
Gary & JoAnn Chambers
SHAPESHIFTER**

Visionary Music

VisionaryMusic.com
evolve@visionarymusic.com
828.301.7410

Copyright © 2001-12 by Gary & JoAnn Chambers

All rights reserved. No part of this book may be reproduced, stored, transmitted or otherwise copied without prior written permission of the publisher. Brief quotations and references may be used with appropriate credit lines.

The information in this book does not replace any professional medical advice nor does it prescribe any treatment for any physical, mental or emotional illness or disease. The content of this book is for spiritual explorers seeking to expand their consciousness by stepping beyond what is commonly considered "normal." This work is to be considered experimental and for those seeking adventures into multidimensional landscapes of the higher realms of Light & Sound. It is up to each individual engaging with this material to be responsible for his or her own welfare and the authors and publishers assume no responsibility for your interpretation of this material. Honor the work and respect the process.

ISBN 1-4421-5913-8
EAN-13 is 978-1-4421-5913-6

First Edition, January 2001
Second Edition, July 2008
Third Edition, May 2009
Fourth Edition, May 2011
Fifth Edition, May 2012
Printed in U.S.A.

Published by CreateSpace.com

*The more I reach out to IT, the more IT reaches back to me.
Modulate the Lifewave of the Body Electric.*
—*Shapeshifter*

Contents

The Place to Begin this Journey	8
Preface: Down the Rabbit Hole – The Red Pill	15
What is DNA Activation?	17
Our Approach to DNA Activation	19
Activating DNA via Multidimensional Sound	23
Exploring Frequency Spectrums	26
Building & Expanding Frequency Range	29
LevelOne DNA Activation	31
Unfolding Teaching from a Sonic Mystery School	32
Truth Emerging within Sound	34
Blending with other Programs & Teachings	35
Active vs. Passive Listening	37
Expanding your Consciousness	40
12 Strands & Beyond	41
A Journey into the Land of Science	47
Effects & Benefits of DNA Activation using our Multidimensional Music	57
Listening Suggestions	60
About the Creators	73
The Creation Begins	74
Pre-Activation/Recapitulation Journal	78

A Note from the Authors . . . .

We are continually updating our websites, adding new information and resources on the subject of DNA Activation, Sound Healing and our Multidimensional Music. Be sure that we have your most recent email address to be notified of these updates. If you are not already signed up to receive our email news send us your email address to get on this list. We will keep you updated on our latest postings to our website, new CDs and products that we release and keep you up to date on our various projects. Visit our blog at Shapeshifterblog.com to see What's New. If you want to talk with us about this work and your experiences, please call us at 828.301.7410 or email Shapeshifter at evolve@VisionaryMusic.com.

DNA I AND ?

this, the first, the place to start
feeling tones of alchemy's art
in the memory of the cells
is the key
multi-dimensional, infinite, free
that which leads to immortality
pulsing modulation resonates within
to the heart of the matter
is where we begin

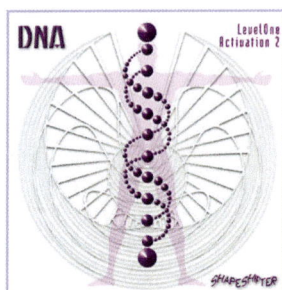

in this, the second
we enter into the depths profound
through waveforms of evolving sound
energetic seals dissolve
light quotient's creativity unbound
electrons expanding orbits revolve
in freedoms dance again
in the full spectrum of the transmission we send
all together, more than the sum of each alone
a calling and a journey home

in this, the third
an energetic balance made,
communication and communion beyond words
a bridge links gaia, human, alien and the divine
a common ground beyond space and time
for, in truth, all emanate from same
different aspects of the game
lines of probability converge
past, present and future merge
in the point of power
the nexus of the now
synchronicities and infinite possibilities emerge

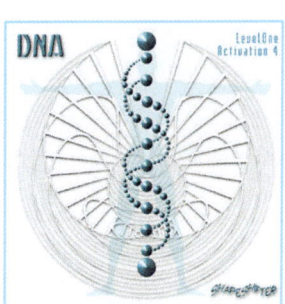

in this, the fourth
a vision of rebirth
descending into the element of earth
our path of intent leads underground
to hidden treasures revealed in sound
in these dark caverns formed in tears
of many lives and many years
we face our deepest doubts and fears
the way transformed in love's delight
dispells the pall of illusion's night

IT has been our joy and our divine gift to bring forth these DNA Activation soundscapes at this wondrous time in humanity's current evolutionary timeline. The information in this accompanying book expands upon the vast multidimensional knowledge that is contained within the soundscapes, as well as presenting you with the nuts and bolts of the process. The entire experience is dependent upon your sincere intent to be activated, which is the first step of this journey. In this book, we will share with you our current body of work as it relates to the LevelOne DNA Activation Series - how they were created, what their purpose can be in your life and how to use them. We will also include a little of the meta-science and theories behind our work. We encourage you to expand your studies of this subject further as there are many others on the planet offering excellent information on this research. The more you understand about their creation, the more powerful the effects of your listening experiences can become. The information presented in this guide is written for beginners as well as those who have been exploring related topics for some time. These topics would include spiritual healing & transformational work, conscious evolution, metaphysics, spiritual philosophy, sound healing, ancient alchemy and modern day quantum physics and more. The writings come forth in several ways; as channeled teachings received from our higher guidance team, our personal studies and our research with many clients in our private practice. Primarily this information emanates from our extensive explorations with the DNA soundscapes throughout our own transformational process. We've been working with these channeled sonic transmissions since 1986 and are as honored to receive them as we were to be a part of the creation process. They have been a true friend during these challenging times of our planet's transition into the higher realms of Light. They will assist you in moving your primary focus from the 3rd dimensional reality into the 5th World/Heaven on Earth manifestations. They assist in the ascension process by aligning you, at all times, with the 2012-23 frequencies pouring on to the planet daily.

   This LevelOne series is only the beginning of what will be a marvelous adventure into the transformational process from a carbon based human into a multidimensionally aware crystalline being of Light, infused with the unlimited abundance of the Universe. Those who have worked with the LevelOne series and feel ready to move on to the DNA L2 Series can take the next steps to accelerate their work on the planet. So much more will be learned as this adventure continues and we always remain open to the magic and mystery as it unfolds. If you consider yourself an explorer on the fringes of the expanding consciousness movement, then this work will be one of those tools that you engage with often to facilitate the increase of Light energy in your being. As your knowledge and intuitive understanding of sound, light, vibration and frequency continues to evolve, the more you will understand the power within these soundscapes to assist you on your evolutionary journey.

   Our name, Shapeshifter, reflects the ever changing (shapeshifting), evolving aspects of us and our work. At the core of our creative works is sound, which we have learned to shift the shape of through modern technology and ancient teachings of profound implications. As you come to know us through our growing body of work, you will know that you are a part of the Shapeshifter energy too.

         Welcome to our Sonic Mystery School, Enjoy your journeys!
         Gary & JoAnn Chambers

The Place to Begin this Journey

Read this section before listening to DNA Activation Soundscapes

We suggest that you read through this Companion Guide before you fully engage with the soundscapes. Consider this the first level of initiation into this vast multidimensional sonic mystery school filled with magical and wondrous adventures. By reading the guide first, it provides the mental body with a bridge to step out further into the unknown realms of Light. For some, this mental form of knowledge may not be necessary, but for others, it will be the difference in truly understanding what this work is all about and how it can assist you on your current evolutionary path.

As with anything we share with you, it is important to remember that we are fellow travellers who are seeking answers to many of the same questions you are pondering. Use your own guidance system to navigate through the word and sound pictures that we are relaying to you from our personal explorations. We suggest that you use discernment, self reflection and conduct a fair amount of research before you engage with any program that offers you assistance on your spiritual journey, including ours. We offer you many avenues for learning more about us and our work before you decide to go deeper with these offerings. Be sure to request the free intro PDF info if you have not already done so.

Some of the information in this opening section is expanded upon in the guide, but for our purpose here, we wanted to give you a quick overview so that you can get started on this amazing adventure without delay.

- Everyone is at a different juncture on their evolutionary path, which will greatly affect how your experiences with these soundscapes will unfold. Some people will have an amazing shift and awakening in the first listening session, while for others it can take some time for these new sounds to marinate in your field of awareness enough to cause noticeable shifts. Some may even have an adverse reaction to these higher frequencies as they stream into your environment to raise the Light. Anything of a denser or darker nature will rise up in protest initially which may require some conscious intervention on your part to clear and resolve before moving on. This density can take the form of foods, people, places and activities that you are currently engaged with. Examine them carefully to determine which are holding aspects of negativity in your life and then make the necessary adjustments to shift to a more positive reflection. For your first deep listening session, we recommend you follow the guidelines in our

Listening Suggestions section of this guide - see #1 - The First Time (page 63)

- We will present you with a wide range of information so that you can extract that which is specific to your path at this time. As you continue to immerse yourself more deeply into these sounds, you should come back to this companion guide and re-read it again so that you can unfold more of the multidimensional teachings that are offered here. For your first reading, we suggest you go through it while listening to the DNA #1 soundscape playing quietly in the background. The music will enhance your learning and absorption of this material on many different levels. If you come to sections where you are not quite sure what is being shared, just read it and allow the information to be assimilated on the higher levels. The next time you re-read the guide, new vistas of meaning will arise within you because you will have engaged with the frequencies.

- DNA Activation is not something to be taken lightly or without respect for the process. It is not part of the get it quick type programs that are available in today's self-help market. It is a lifelong journey of dedication and the soundscapes can be available to support you continuously throughout this process. This program is meant for the more mature spiritual traveller who has done at least some developmental work on themselves in the area of psychology, emotional release, body cleansing/detoxing, self awareness and spiritual development programs. The process can enhance these areas, so some previous knowledge of what is happening is always helpful to avoid confusion or concern about the various steps and stages that one goes through on this journey. The soundscapes provide a steady stream of higher frequencies into your energetic matrix. The more you can take, the more it will release. This allows for a slow, steady unfolding that is actually an accelerated path because of the consistency attained. Consistency is very important to your results. If you are feeling off balance or your 3D world is reflecting disharmony, then back off a bit on the process until you feel the integration has occurred. The music will always reflect back at you what is going on in your life that needs attention. You will learn to engage with the music as a guide or a personal therapist to help understand what is taking place in your reality. When we say back off, we mean to play them quietly in the background but don't engage with them deeply. When you engage deeply, you play them louder and are in a meditative state with full awareness placed on your intentions and the becoming the music technique. If you have not done the "Become The Music" guided journey, see our website homepage or get the AYD (Activate Your DNA) #2 DVD Training program (see back of guide). These images on the next page will offer you the basic idea.

DNA Activation/Shapeshifter

MUSIC · LISTENING TO MUSIC · FEELING THE MUSIC · BECOME THE MUSIC · DISSOLVE

- DNA Activation is not a quick solution for emotional problems, health issues, blocked creativity, financial issues nor an immediate release of intuitive/psychic gifts. Although for some, this can be fairly immediate, again depending on where you are on your journey when you come to these soundscapes. All these manifestations take considerable time, patience, perseverance and dedication in order to fully attain. Small steps on a consistent basis will lead to the success of any of these intentions. As you get more focused about the things you want to attain, it is important to set clear intentions. Once you do this, the frequencies in the soundscapes start to align the pieces of the puzzle in all the dimensional realms to manifest this for you. Your active participation will be required in order to make room for this to occur, which may mean many things will change in your current life in order to allow them to actualize. This can be moving to a new location, changing relationships and jobs, selecting foods that are more enlivening to your body temple and becoming fully responsible for all your actions. All your current and previous belief systems will come up for review as you engage with this process, so remain open, flexible and always in a state of awe at the magic that unfolds in your reality. Be ever attuned to the messages and synchonicities that start to appear in your life. The musical soundscapes will become an ever evolving soundtrack on this adventure, as if it was scored specifically for the daily activities of your life. Follow these sonic flows by letting go more and more into the mystery of life.

- Our initial suggestion is to listen to each CD at least 7 times before moving on to the next for your initial pass through the 4 soundscapes. This means 7 times in a deepened state of meditation, fully focused on engaging with the sounds, pretty much throughout the entire soundscape. This also means that you are not just passively listening in the process, but that you are shamanically journeying with the various levels and layers of your consciousness, using your intent to direct the flows of information. Do some more research on this as well as reviewing Suggestion #2 - Shamanic Journeying in the Listening Suggestions section of this guide (see page 64). This doesn't mean 7 times as background music or 7 times without your full attention on the process or falling asleep in the middle. Each time you work with the music, you should set some sort of initial intent, whether it is specific or broad in scope is not important initially. You will refine things as you move along the process. This starts to set energy in motion to conspire around your energetic matrix by sending out focused desires into the greater Universal Energy Field/Source. Pay attention, as these connections will start to come into your field as synchronicities. You can adjust your listening times as you feel guided, again these are just our suggestions based on our experiences. The idea is to let these new frequencies integrate into your life in a way in which it seems somewhat seamless, but yet there is awareness that something is shifting and changing around you. People will respond differently to you and you will notice things on subtle levels that you didn't notice before. Once you have gotten through all 4 CDs for the first pass, you can then listen in any order that you want. As you go back through them, they will continue to shift and change as you do by releasing new sounds that your emerging Light body is able to hear. This is an indication that you are evolving and taking in more Light.

- A very common thing that occurs is a natural flushing of toxins in the body. Rather than bring on a healing crisis like a cold, flu or virus type experience, we recommend you consider starting a cleansing program along with your initial passage through these soundscapes. There are many great programs out there today that are comprehensive in scope. Try to find one that uses organic and wildcrafted herbs in their blends. Consult with a professional if you do not have previous experience with detoxing programs. If you do get some symptoms, you might back off on the soundscapes a bit and just let it run its course. Over time you will learn how to deal with this in a holistic, self healing way. Detoxing should become a regular process in your life from here on. We do them quarterly as a way to keep up with the toxins we take in from the environment. Clean up your diet and start to remove things that are more connected to a denser reality - preservatives, chemicals, processed, genetically engineered - you get the picture. Another aspect of this detoxing is that at times you will require extra deep sleep, sometimes 10-12 hours at a time. Depending on your previous stress levels, this could go on for some time. Do what you can to allow your body to go through this process without adding artificial or synthetic stimulants. In time, you will actually need less sleep, but you will need to go through that detoxing phase first.

- On the spiritual journey, there are many paths to follow. We encourage you to find the ones that hold the most truth for you and then be open to change as you evolve. This work is not a teaching per se, it is a way to help you access these higher realms more easily and to bring back the teachings you discover in your journeys. It is a mystery school of sound that allows you, the listener, to discover the teachings within. If you do not feel you have a good spiritual foundation, we offer a DVD Training Program, called AYD - Shamanic Journeys into the Multidimensional Timestrea (AYD=Activate Your DNA), to help you develop some of the basic skills needed. AYD #1 helps you to balance your chakras, expand your auric field, connect with higher guidance and activate your DNA. If you are new to sound healing and working with sound for transformational processes, then there is a DVD to help you learn how to work with sound. AYD #2 helps you to work with our multidimensional music and sound on a deeper level. From learning how to become the music, it then goes on to teach you more about working directly with your energy body and learning how to become an energetic being of Light by using sound to access those teachings.

• Always know that we are here to support you as you move along your journey with these soundscapes. We offer a variety of ways for you to interact with us from teleconferences to live chat and spiritual guidance sessions at The 3rd Eye website (see back of guide for more info). The DNA LevelOne series is the place to begin, to create a foundation upon which you can build a stable spiritual body of Light. All the other soundscapes in our catalog will assist you in specific areas of focus. DNA 1.5 is the bridge to take when you are ready to begin the L2 series. When you receive the impulses to take the next steps, we will be here to assist you. The DNA L2 (LevelTwo) program (see back of guide) is something you can consider once you have spent time integrating the LevelOne frequencies. As for how long that may take, each person is different. For someone with a lot of previous experience before engaging with them, this could be 6 months or less. For those totally new to this process of unfolding, it can be several years. You can talk with us to determine where you are on this journey.

• One of the things that will emerge from listening to the music is a deepening awareness of your pastlives. The music will start to bring some of these lives to the forefront of your consciousness via dreams or deju vu experiences. It is not important that you uncover all of them, but there are some key ones that are important to your journey. Some of these will be empowering initially and some will be disempowering for you to own up to. As you work through these key lifetimes you will see how those imprints have been controlling many of your actions and reactions in life. The music will release various sounds that will trigger these memories within the cellular levels. As these are cleared and released, the music will shift from something that may have sounded discordant to something that is totally divine. This is another sign to let you know that you are making progress. The music will constantly show you what is happening throughout your multidimensional selves and what it needs in order to bring it into balance and alignment. If you want assistance with your pastlives, we offer readings at The Third Eye.

• As for the listening systems that you should listen to these soundscapes with, we recommend that you get as high a quality system as you can – woofer, midrange and tweeter. Because these are done with a very wide range of high and low frequencies, you will want a system that can give you the most fidelity possible. We realize not everyone is going to run out and buy a new stereo, but it is something you might want to work towards as you start to engage more deeply with sound as a transformational tool. We recommend an external speaker system as opposed to headphones predominantly. This is because we want your etheric bodies to experience the music as well as your entire environment. Good quality headphones can still be used with excellent results in the brain/mind whole brain balancing area. You can convert the CDs to MP3s, but remember that you are compressing the files and losing quite a bit of the necessary frequencies – use them for casual listening only. Just be sure that you are also listening on a full range stereo system as well for your deeper shamanic sessions. If you want to make the files smaller for your Ipod type players, use FLAC or Apple Lossless. Just do your best to experience them on a high end sound system to really get the full benefit. If you ever have an opportunity to play the CDs on a sound table, do it. You will be amazed at the amount of movement you will experience and spacial quality of the sound all around you. You can also visit us in Florida and experience the music in our Odyssey Sound & Light Temple. Contact JoAnn when you are making your travel plans to set up your session.

Above all, be playful and enjoy your journeys with these soundscapes. There are no hard and fast rules or things you are supposed to experience. Everyone of us is a unique work of art and so everyone is going to engage with these frequencies in a different way. Let go, relax and engage in the magical world of multidimensional sound.

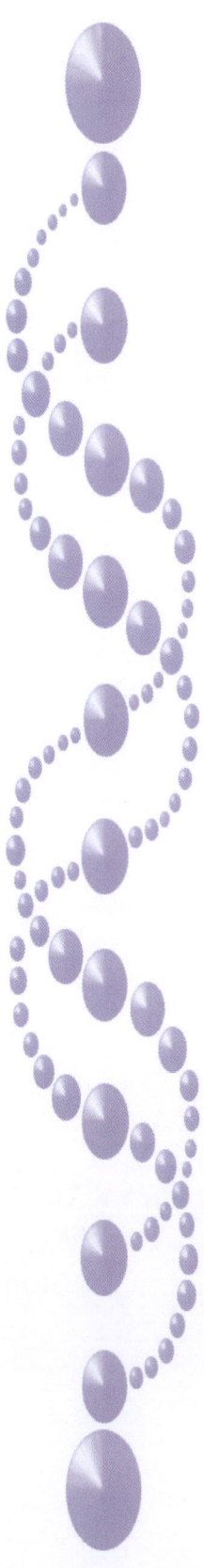

DNA Activation/Shapeshifter

PREFACE: Down the Rabbit Hole - The Red Pill

Each person must ultimately decide their role as a Lightworker and how far down the rabbit hole they are willing to go in this lifetime. If you know in your heart that you are here at this time to be participating player in the transition from 3D/4D to 4D/5D realms, the you know you have to go as far down as it goes. All roles are valued, whether it is a leadership role or a supporting role. You are either here to do this work or you are not, it will be pretty clear to you. There are many tasks that are part of this process that don't require you to give your entire life over to this mission. If you have large extended families, children, complex business obligations that require your attention as a central player, then there is great reason for that to have appeared in your life at this time and you must tend to that in order to move to the next step. As in any project, there are many roles to be played. Some do the work, some do the planning and some provide the resources. Do your part, whatever form that takes.

This DNA Activation approach is for those who know deep in their heart that they are here to assist in bridging the energetic pathways from the 3rd dimension to a 5th dimensional reality. It is coded in your DNA to be a part of this wave of energy and many of you have already begun your activation process either through our soundscapes, a workshop/teacher/healer or by setting your own intent to make it so. The DNA soundscapes will provide you with the frequency maps you will need in order to build the roadways to navigate this multidimensional terrain. It is a labyrinth of vast proportions and you will come to find this music provides you with a way to focus some of this energy and move with greater ease through the gateways as they are opened up by those who are riding the crest of this wave. Activation is only the beginning step, actualization will take many years of dedication and focus to fully embody and become a multi-stranded being of Light. It has been proven that which one focuses time and attention towards, manifests. By holding a consistent state of soft intention on DNA Activation throughout all aspects of your life, you release the chemical processes within your cells that carries the information enabling you to step into and become the next evolution of mankind. This includes the complete unification and balance of the body, mind, emotional & spiritual matrix.

Consider this analogy for a moment, think of the history of the planet, any version. You know that life started off in groups scattered throughout various locations around the globe. Over time man ventured out beyond their borders creating pathways into unknown territory. Roads were built, waterways were mapped, airways were chartered – all to build the geographical maps so that we all could easily know how to get from point A to point B. It is now without question or thought that you would look at a map to go from California to Florida or the US to England. As the matrix of existence that we currently consider our world (3D/4D) expands to include etheric space (5D+) and the realms in which we are able to exist, hold focus and venture forth into, become our new reality, multidimensional maps of this territory will need to be created to assist those who choose to follow this path. Sound is one common element that can merge/blend/unify these pathways. Multidimensional sounds will create the maps that we need to traverse this new World of Light.

These expanded realms are not easily mapped using current 3D forms of navigation protocols, they are not solid (not that anything really is) and cannot be mapped using the same tools or techniques as were used to map earths terrain. It is not ultimately a mental process, it is one that will rely heavily on our expanded senses to achieve any sort of comprehension. The mental realm has served a great purpose in leading us to this point in our evolution, but it is time for this to shift, imperative really, as our survival as a species depends upon it. Our methods of attaining knowledge and wisdom from current academic structures is now limited and becoming outmoded in exchange for quicker ways to download greater amounts of information in less time. The shaman within each person will need to rise back up, so as to be able to fully comprehend the hows and whys of what this means to our consensus reality as it was and what it is to become. We are all shamans and we are all shapeshifters; able to use our inner compass to navigate etheric realms via our energetic connection to All that exists in our Universe. The term God will too become limited in the scope of what the core of our existence really is. As the navigable dimensions become even more etheric in nature, we must develop the physical vehicles that can move about in those realms. This is why it is important for you to build your body of Light — your Lightbody. Music/Sound, composed and channeled forth with conscious intent, is one of the most powerful tools we currently have available to map these new destinations. Just like roadways and railways were built to provide passageways for people and resources to move about, we are building sonic roadways for lightworkers to traverse galactic space. It is time now for this knowledge to come forth and for those starseeds to fully actualize their full potentials to be the wayshowers for humanity. The ascension teachings of Jesus and other great masters has now reached enough minds and hearts in humanity for us to achieve this goal as a large collective movement en mass.

Your willingness to go deeper into your inner self explorations will be necessary in order to bring forth your brightest expression of the divine. The intensity of the Light in the higher realms will quite literally burn you out if you are not able to embrace and hold the higher frequencies within your personal bioenegetic matrix. Darkness and density cannot exist in these realms and those who would try to seek to enter these places will be quickly turned away until they can sustain a consistent state of higher vibration. The music we create provides you with the energetic sustenance that will gradually and steadily increase the Light Quotient in your bioenergtic form, enabling you to accrete the Light needed to hold a consistent state of focus as you traverse the higher realms. This is paramount to the development of your Lighbody.

This all requires great changes in your life, which do not happen overnight. You can move forward at a quickening pace, but you still have to take the time to process and integrate the new frequencies as they fully take hold in your life. This will show up in all areas of your life that have to then be reviewed, examined carefully as to their necessity and purpose and then shifted to a higher vibrational pattern reflective of the new levels of Light that you will then embody. These changes affect your work and career path, the location on the planet in which you are living, your relationship to your family and friends and how you treat the physical form that you find yourself in residence. It is like being called to service, but not really knowing from the beginning what the end result will look like. This in itself is a huge step away from the current paradigm of living ones life. A lot of trust and faith is going to be required of you that goes way beyond conventional forms of religious teachings. IT is not a path for those who want to play it safe and value security above all else. There are many challenges and risks to take along the way that test your resolve and commitment to walk on this path. The reward or promise at the end of the road (there really isn't an end) is nebulous at best. However the divine spark within you tells you constantly that all that you do is purposeful and that you somehow agreed to all of this on another dimension of reality long ago. You will know deep in your heart that you can do nothing else but to walk this path and continue to move forward steadily committed to the higher purpose of assisting Earth's humanity in its current evolutionary phase of ascension.

If you know in your heart that this is your journey this lifetime, then we invite you to join us in a grand adventure. We have been fully committed to riding this path for over 20 years (since 1986) and have gained a lot of knowledge and wisdom along the way. Still much is yet to be learned and discovered and we remain ever humble and open to the mysteries that await. We have found the soundscapes to be one of the most powerful and tangible teachers on this journey, as they reveal to us new levels as we are ready. You will learn, as we have, that there are many layers of information folded within space and time contained in our DNA that are released when you are ready. There will be times that you will receive a download of information that comes through as transmissions of multidimensional information. You will come to know how to unravel this information through the process we call "LIFE"–Living In Full Expression.

Are you ready for the "Red Pill?"

What is DNA Activation?

DNA Activation can be considered a concept, a theory, a philosophy, a technique, a process or all of the above, depending on how one decides to engage with it. But mostly it is a grand adventure unlike any you have ventured on before. As a concept, it is a declaration of strong intent to awaken one's dormant potentials within the multidimensional human DNA codex. It is a technique that enables one to activate aspects of the 97% junk DNA in the 2 strand DNA as well as

What you seek was inside you all of the time – inside your DNA, a place called HOME.

to consciously tap into the strands that exist in the higher dimensional realms of Light. The initial activation experience is merely the first step of a very long journey, which ultimately takes years and lifetimes to truly embrace. By consciously initiating the DNA Activation process within oneself, you can awaken many of the gifts and talents that have been waiting for you to be ready to actualize them. These can include self healing abilities, healing assistance for others, clairvoyance/audience/sentience, intuitive/ESP/psychic abilities, creative expressions, conscious generation of synchronicities, miracles and the manifestation of Abundance on all levels. Whatever talents you may have spent time developing in other lifetimes may also surface as a result of your awakening process based on your new ability to generate higher levels of joy and happiness in your life, which always leads to a higher level of creative expression. When one truly shines forth their creativity out in the World in tangible forms, their financial abundance also increases as the exchange of energy with Source flows back and forth continuously through all things of an expanded nature. The more you create, the more you connect, the more flow you will experience. It is unlimited.

If viewed from a scientific theory perspective, you can consider this work to be a part of the studies in future science now evolving in the quantum physics labs across the planet. In the wondrous body human, the "double serpent" DNA strands within the nucleus of each cell, if stretched end to end, would be over 125 billion miles long. This biotechnology contains over a hundred trillion times as much information as our most sophisticated storage devices. DNA is composed of a hyper sophisticated language within the 2 genomes and their backup copies contained in each human cell. Within the genomes, the dual ribbon DNA winds around itself forming 23 chromosomes in two pairs. The total genetic information, within these structures, is a sequence of over 6 billion base pairs or 12 billion "letters." The code for the proteins and enzymes, the genes, represents roughly only 3 percent of the mapped human genome. The function of the remaining 97% is as yet unknown to conventional science — they are working on it. We believe that the repeat sequences of this 97% contain coded information to evolve the energetic structure of the body human, spirit in form. It is our sincere intent to activate this dormant information through the higher vibrational energy of sound, to "Modulate The Lifewave."

The additional 10-strand dimensional states that we are working towards, exist as interpenetrating overlays in the more subtle realms of vibration and frequency.

As you read this information, be sure to put on the DNA CDs in the background to help you assimilate the information on all levels. We begin with some of the basic information about this subject and then we'll go deeper into some of the more esoteric teachings related to this work.

Many different teachings and philosophies have been rising up in this area of study since we first began our research work in 1989. The term "DNA Activation" really started moving around in metaphysical circles starting in the late 90s/early 2000, mostly in the internet communities, simply because it was time for humanity to wake up and start to claim their divinity and release themselves from agreed upon limitations. There are many stories and legends being told about the origins of this kind of work along with many different techniques and tools created to facilitate the process.

This music is channeled from a place of pure intent and can be a multi-dimensional resource of evolutionary knowledge and wisdom.

There are many channels who have brought through information about the reasons why our DNA was limited to 2 strands that are interesting and enlightening to become aware of. We encourage you to explore these teachings with an open mind, feel into what feels to be a deep truth for you and then move on into doing the actual work. Our focus and purpose in this field is to offer you a powerful tool for awakening this dormant DNA. We are not here to give you historical data or information on the shadow government or alien agendas regarding the manipulation of our DNA, but if you engage with the soundscapes deep enough, this information along with much more will be revealed to you as it has been shared with us through our experience. We are interested in actualization and results here in the 3rd dimensional (3D) realms as this is where we currently hold our primary focus. We feel there is great importance in grounding these principles into tangible actions and results, turning them into projects and manifestations of profound teachings on the planet. We, as starseeds and lightworkers, came here to actualize this energy into solid, substantial forms to assist all of humanity on the journey of awakening. DO what you came here to DO. We encourage you to remain open and in a continual state of wonder and awe. As you do this consistently more of who you are and what you are here to do will be revealed to you. Allow the DNA Activation process using our soundscapes to become a regular part of your life so that you are continually involved in an adventure that is raising your vibrational essence each day with the acceleration frequencies that are in alignment with the 2012 ascension timeline.

> *These chakric gateways connect a vast matrix of interpenetrating Harmonic Universes in many dimensional states.*

Our Approach to DNA Activation

Sound is the fabric of our entire existence. Each of us is an expression of our own personal symphony of sound. Each individual life could be scored like a movie soundtrack. Many are stuck in a groove playing the same old song with slight variations, over and over and over again throughout the entire course of their life. Oliver Wendell Holmes said "Most people go to their graves with their music inside them." These soundscapes invite you to play your song, a new song, many new songs, by learning how to become sound in action.

> *As your encoded information is released, it will flood the cells with vital energy, raising the vibration of the physical, the energy body and beyond.*

Music, sound, modulation, harmonics, vibration and frequencies are fundamental elements emanating "beyond" and through the core level subatomic of the 3rd dimensional level of reality. We are energy beings composed of various oscillating wave forms of frequencies that mesh together to form the matter that we call the human body. A much larger part of who we are exists in the non-visible, etheric realm of energy. What we know to exist in the realm of 3D reality also exists in higher octaves of Light. These interpenetrating layers from the physical to the etheric and beyond reach out into the Universal Oneness and connect us to All That Is. These DNA Activation transmissions were created with the intent to connect these worlds into one multidimensional experience, to create a smooth, seamless transition from one to the other — to build the frequency maps within this vast multi-dimensional territory we call consciousness. Some of the sound patterns in these sonic adventures resonate immediately with the unique energy matrix that is "you," while other sections may be a bit more of a challenge to integrate. This is as it should be, as we are activating first level evolutionary codes within the DNA. Evolution, by its very nature, is not always what you expect.

> *These soundscapes oscilate through the spectrum of manifestation, from the two strands through the etheric harmonic overlays that some have semantically termed the other strands.*

This music may seem simple or complex, rhythmic or ambient, alien or divine. We can assure you that it is a reflection and celebration of you, a gift from the deepest levels of who you are, what you need at this stage in your becoming, so go with the flow with a sense of adventure.

We'll include some brief statements now about our magical DNA — DNA is a bridge between matter and the Divine. It is the awakening journey of a Soul rising up to the higher realms and becoming an Avatar, an Ascended Master of Light in all the various steps and stages along the way. Spend some time thinking about how wondrous the body human truly is, in all its amazing workings and functions. It is the Spiritual Temple of our being, the only place we can reside while holding focus in the 3rd dimension. Our intent is to unlock and activate the codex within the DNA using sound, harmonics, modulation and vibration, thereby connecting frequency spectrums throughout all dimensional realms.

There are many stories and myths of these codes throughout our history, why they are there and a hint of what they might contain. Some talk of "alien" intervention within the timelines of mankinds existence, of the rise and fall of ancient civilizations now shrouded by the mists of time, far more advanced than our own. There is much that all but the most objective and open-minded scientific minds of this world have, in the past, refused to acknowledge. Much is changing and with the accelerating consciousness on this planet much will be revealed as more and more open up to a wider spectrum of information and knowledge. We, on another level, are also learning as the multi-timeline, multi-dimensional tale unfolds. We follow the path with clarity, awareness and intent — then we relay the information to you through these sonic landscapes. This is our mission work during this incarnation as we have done many times before. We lovingly invite you with open arms to join us on this journey of adventures.

We realize that linear thinkers and skeptics may choose to challenge our work and question the theories/concepts in which we base it on. We have found that those who tend to lean strongly towards the mental side of experiencing life, have more difficulty shifting into the multidimensional flows of these soundscapes. After all, it has been primarily taught that factual information only comes from academia and scientific analysis. We are asking you to open up to the possibility that information can be obtained in a non-linear way by consciously connecting to higher frequencies through this multidimensional music. Ultimately this is the awakening of our sixth sense, a new, more expanded, way of experiencing reality. If you tend to travel more in the mental grooves, but you would like to explore this further so as to move towards a balanced state of body, mind, emotion & spirit, then we recommend you get some of the brain/mind whole brain thinking soundscapes on the market today in conjunction with our offerings. This will help to open up the right brain creative thinking mind and allow more possibilities and potentials into your life. We encourage all to use discernment when engaging with any sound based products. Do your research, study the creators/developers and their process to help you find the right place of resonance for where you are in your life at this time. Aligning yourself properly will bring forth a greater knowing of the mystery of all in a more harmonious way throughout all aspects of your life. You will also experience more success in the process if you find the right place of alignment. If one steps into these higher realms before the proper foundation has been built, one might find their life moving into states of chaos and disruption, which might require a considerable amount of time to bring it back into flow. It is better to pace yourself, integrate the knowledge and ground the energy into tangible forms and actions before moving on to each next step. If you follow this process, you will have greater success in all your manifestation goals.

What was Hidden, is now Revealed.

Our path is to bring through this work with as much clarity as we can without the need to analyze and measure within current scientific confines. We encourage those of you who are here to bring that form of knowledge forth, to take this work and analyze away. Science and Spirituality can support each other on this journey of our collective evolution and if allowed to do so with more freedom, humanity will only benefit from these collaborations. Observe, define and explore our creative output and its effects on human biology, physiology and psychology to the depths that you can. While we engage in the science, for the most part, we are shamanic travelers, intuitives and creatives. There are those on the planet at this time whose consciousness is of a more open, objective nature that will enjoy exploring our output from a more expanded approach. It is to those of you that we extend a warm welcome to research and explore. Let's review the results from a space of collaboration and mutual respect for each others gifts.

Certain resonant frequencies have profound effects on the codes within the DNA, keys that have been waiting for thousands, perhaps millions of years for the right evolutionary sequence to be activated. As a tuning fork generates waves in the air creating a certain pitched sound, current synthesizer technology is able to create a full-range harmonic spectrum that Modulates the Lifewave and activates the codes. It is no accident that mankind's electronic sound generating devices have evolved to the point where resonant vibratory frequencies can be generated to create these evolutionary currents of energy. In our approach to DNA activation, from the information given to and through us, our sincere intent is to raise the vibration of the physical to a more expanded level, reaching the full potential of spirit manifest in matter. There is a purpose, beyond the learning of lessons, as to why humanity has chosen to adopt and adapt to incarnate forms; to hold focus in a human body. The secret to this mission, of why we are really here, is in the very heart of matter itself.

DNA Activation/Shapeshifter

The sonic key will fit the lock; the veils will be lifted. As the encoded information is released it will flood the cells with vital energy, raising the vibration of the physical, the energy body and beyond. Those who make the conscious choice will reach a new level of expression — a new level of the Game of Life. In gentle stages, so the process will integrate with who you are — as much as you can handle and no more. This occurs under your free will and directed by your sincere intent. It's not about ascending off the planet, but about fully becoming while still incarnate in physical form.

Resonance leads to an implicate higher order. Instead of repairing something that is dis-eased, our approach is to simply invoke this higher blueprint — a more expansive state of spontaneous re-generation. If you want to live an extended life, to youth yourself or become physically immortal by mastering the ascension process, it is possible if you can truly believe on all levels of your being. If you seek unlimited abundance and freedom, more flow, to awaken, to be fully alive, to open to more love and enlightened relationships, this is all possible and more. Accept your connection with All That Is, intend these things, accept the wonder of what you are and begin to believe. Your active participation is required. This LevelOne DNA Activation Series we offer you will begin to prepare you for the more profound stages of individual and collective evolution yet to be revealed. To integrate the true energy of transformation, you must fully embrace that which you are. Go as far as you choose to go, you control the stop, start, pause, horizontal and vertical flow.

We create these enveloping soundscapes with the highest intent and an empathic connection to All That Is. These compositions are therefore created in a sacred space of being and for the empowerment and enlightenment of all. Because you each have free will, you always have the choice of how deeply you immerse yourself (by this we refer to the aware personality matrix), into the vibrational space we have created. Yes, we are activating a higher level, more integrated energy field not only within your inner being but also in your outer environment as well — into your living space, your place of work — wherever these soundscapes are played. Consider the positive implications of this information. Harmony, expansion and an increased quotient of Light will uplift your vibration and therefore through resonance, the vibration of those around you. As a result, your interaction with the world will flow in increasing harmony. New opportunities will manifest in more attunement to your heart's desires. Synchronistic events will emerge in your ongoing Vision Quest and you will live a life full of wonder and magic each day.

> When we travel inward, we invoke, with intent, the energy of integration and the coming together of all dimensions of experience within the Body Temple.

How can all of this happen from just listening to a soundscape, you may ask! Well, it can't. Not by playing the CDs as if they are background musical wallpaper. There is no magic wand that anyone can wave over your head and suddenly everything in your life has transformed without any consciously directed intent, without any active participation on your part. Nothing of true and lasting value ever works that way. Again, the factor of free will comes into play. You must make the inner decision to lovingly immerse yourself and trust in the process because you wish to move forward, to transcend

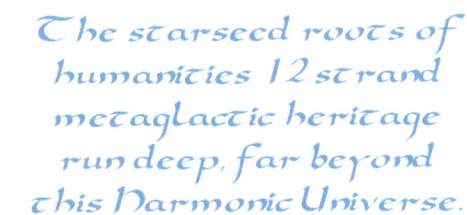

The starseed roots of humanities 12 strand metaglactic heritage run deep, far beyond this Harmonic Universe.

inertia, to grow, evolve, whatever you term it. If you do so, your intent will connect with these sonic teachings and your potentials will unfold — the possible becomes real. Real to the level that you are willing to direct your consciousness to have that which you desire to manifest within your reality. Belief is a powerful key, as it is in all things. We create a pool, a reservoir of energy attuned to the common ground of a shared planetary vibration; you use it in a positive manner how you will. We have no ultimate agenda, nothing for you to join or become a devotee of.

There is only one real catch, if you choose to call it a catch. Because we have created this music in connection with the planetary Higher Self, the planetary Logos and for the highest good of all concerned, you cannot use the energy generated for manipulation or influence of other beings or situations against their will to achieve a desired goal. This is simply not possible within the framework, however expansive, of this shared adventure. This works both ways in the equation. We, as the channel Shapeshifter, cannot and will not use this energy to manipulate or coerce you in any way, on any level. We have our own adventure; our own aspect of the Game to commune with Source that is far beyond such power plays. All are one, what affects the one, in some way affects all. What we give, we do so out of Higher Love, clearness of intent, respect for the unique being that you are and the acquired experience gained from many lifetimes on this path. What we want for you, is for you to become the fullness of the divinity that you are in all the various facets of that expression.

So again, within these few conditions, use these offerings of energy for your empowered growth and manifestation as you will, in alignment with your soul's path of becoming. You will find that the music changes over time. Each time that you listen, you may pick up new sounds that you didn't hear before. This is because your own vibrational pattern is changing and shifting as you evolve. The things that you focus on will be different. The multi-dimensional mirror of vibrational content within the music will reveal new facets for your enlightenment and exploration. You will begin to notice a shift in your 3D world activities as well. Many new insights will come to Light that were right in front of you the whole time, but you were not able to see them clearly. Your intuition will also increase in alignment with your true unfoldment, as will your ability to manifest all your dreams and desires.

Activating DNA via Multidimensional Sound

A little education on your DNA from a more linear perspective would be appropriate. We are not going to go into this information at great length now, but recommend that you study some additional texts on this subject, if you would like to become more knowledgeable in this area.

Shapeshifter is composed of old souls, on and off world, who have worked with sound concepts for many lifetimes. The power and importance of using sound to activate the multidimensional DNA codex emanates from the ancient mystery schools when sound was understood as a tool for transformational processes. This knowledge is also utilized in many off-world systems as a technique for transmuting the initiate into an adept and ultimately a master. Our incarnational influences are early tribal, Toltec Shamanic, Atlantean, Egyptian/Roman, East Indian, Elemental Realms blended with advanced alien and interdimensional starseed information. We bring forth this knowledge at this particular time in mankind's evolutionary cycle to Modulate The Lifewave and to share with those who are awakening the harmonics of the new sonic landscape. These new realms are considered 5th world frequencies or that which manifests the reality of Heaven on Earth. The higher technology of using sound to activate the DNA codex was known in the ancient mists of history but has been suppressed/lost due to the energetic seals placed upon, and disassembly of, our DNA strands by various influences. As for the sources of this method of control, we will leave you to study the many conspiracy theories available today. Ultimately at this point, it is somewhat irrelevant. What is important is that you GET this and understand that you can break out of this control based construct and reclaim your divinity.

Because some of the more esoteric effects of the soundscapes are not viewable by the limitations of current known earth technology, many of the deep level changes that occur cannot be conclusively and quantitatively measured by observing A+B+C in a linear scientific format. Even though the strands reintegrate on other dimensional octaves, they do link up and are eventually re-integrated into the two strand DNA structure which can be observed by current science. This means that change could be verified with appropriate protocols. At this time, we cannot give you laboratory validation regarding what is occurring in this process until the seals placed upon these energetic states are dissolved. We encourage those who are researching such things, if they even have the tools to record such esoteric energies and their core level effects, as well as the consciousness and openness to know how and where to look to study these frequencies further. A more enlightened, more objective scientific-intuitive current is emerging now on the planet, so we feel the tools will or are being created to explore these possibilities. Our approach is to be considered experimental, pre scientific validation stage. We believe these energy transmissions to be valid, effective and life affirming based on our personal experience and our private research with thousands of clients over the course of 20+ years. As with most of the leading edge information now being received on the planet, much of this ultimately has to be assimilated by a leap of faith and in the spirit of adventure. There are many gifted intuitives and clairvoyants who can validate the effects by reading the auric field or scanning the energy bodies. We have done this ourselves and know the technique to be valid based on positive results. We

> *These organizing matrixes of biophotonic Light, The Language of Light, is the self organizing communication network that connects the levels of manifest reality through the varioius states and dimensions.*

have verified through quarterly chakra portraits and aura readings (available at The 3rd Eye - see back of guide) that positive effects are consistent with using these soundscapes. Use your intuition and discernment to know if this DNA Activation process is for you, do your research. Sense the loving intent behind these words and the centered focus of our work, then decide for yourself.

Your chakras are doorways into multiple worlds and dimensions.

You live, you breathe, your atomic matrix is particles/waves of dancing energy held together in an orchestrated gestalt of awareness. It is unique, yet it reflects a connected focus of energies and dimensions of meaning, emotions and feelings. You trust and believe in this process, in the beating of your heart, the pumping of your blood and the electrical impulses that travel through your neuronal and synaptic structure. You accept the glorious miracle of that reality, a conviction that at the very deepest level within you allows the co-creative artistic expression that is YOU to maintain a coherent, cohesive form. Now stretch your consciousness a bit more and entertain the possibility that your DNA is a receiver, a transmitter and the Grail that holds the Living Light and information of all the myriad dimensions that you are and are connected to.

The validation that you, the explorer, will receive from the energy in these soundscapes will be in the positive effects and gifts that you allow yourself to experience and integrate into your life. As you start to awaken the dormant potentials within your DNA, you will require new sustenance for the physical body in order to move forward in your ascension process and/or building your Light Body, in alignment with the greater planetary unfoldment and initiation. As you start to perceive and accept with radiant full body awareness, that you are composed of vibrational fields of energy, you will come to understand that sound and frequency become part of the food that feeds this energy vessel. When we explore this dance of energy on a fundamental level, in what some scientifics term dark matter/superluminal matter beyond the subatomic, we find DNA and the cellular matrix arising from the intersecting wave interactions; scalar fields of consciousness that resonate, respond and form new implicate orders of awareness from the patterns of these relational coordinates because they emanate from same. Higher consciously created sound becomes one source of our food.

We are constantly being bombarded with sound, internally and externally, and all of this effects our DNA. Your DNA, in one basic analogy, can be equated to a function like the hard drive of your computer, although of course, many levels of capacity and dimensional complexity beyond this simple metaphor. If you had access to the holographic computer technology available to some of the tentacle branches of our Secret Government, you would have a much better example of how massive amounts of information and shades of meaning can be stored and projected from intersecting beams/geometries of Light. Your DNA accumulates all data and sorts it and catalogs it constantly. It is your personal connection to what has been termed the Akashic Records, containing all data from all of your incarnations, on-world and off-world. It contains links and data to the Matrix of information and conscious experience shared by all sentient life throughout the harmonic Universes — past, present and probable futures. Through sounds/frequencies/modulations, we initiate a contact first with the 2-strand DNA that exists in 3D. From this point, by establishing a progressive pattern of sympathetic resonance, we begin the process of activating what has been termed the 3rd, 4th, 5th, 6th, 7th, 8th, 9th, 10th, 11th and 12th strands of our DNA — we build a frequency map of these dimensional qualities or states. It is like waking up and re-energizing a part of yourself that has always existed, but has been asleep for a very long time. The harmonics that exist between these states is often the most difficult territory to navigate through. They are reflected back as chaotic or dramatic expressions in your daily life. The music softens these gateways, making them more accessible for easier transitions in one's life.

Once you become infused with this new energy, you begin to act, think and talk differently. You take on new meanings to your life, that you really are immortal and that you can accomplish any of the dreams that you desire because the manifestation process of learning how to be in harmonious co-creation with the energy dynamic that is the world of matter becomes so much more clear to you. As your vibratory field expands and stabilizes, you will synchronistically attract what you need to do your chosen work. The limitation of time and space will no longer hold the same meaning for you, which allows you to expand your realm of possibilities tenfold. Understand that all the processes and spiritual growth work you have done thus far, all of them support your DNA Activation process. What you need now is simply to become much more deeply aware of these currents of energy. The DNA Activation soundscapes are an empowering tool and an initiation, that will assist you to put all the pieces of the puzzle together seamlessly, allowing all aspects of your expressions to merge into a focused projection of potent energy.

Biophoton light is stored in the living cells of the organism within the DNA molecules of their nuclei.

Exploring Frequency Spectrums

Each of the 4 soundscapes in the LevelOne series contains a predominant range and spectrum of frequencies. Each successive one builds on the previous soundscape, gradually expanding the harmonic range of energy that can be accessed. By working with all 4 soundscapes, you will fill your bio-energetic matrix with this expanded range of frequencies, so that you can consciously travel in and through multidimensional realms while maintaining a cohesive center.

We recommend that you begin your explorations by listening to DNA #1 at least seven times before moving on. This means 7 times in a deep meditative space where you are fully conscious throughout the soundscape, considered a theta state. Seven is the cycle that our inner guidance has expressed to us that will allow optimal empathic resonance to occur within your biology, within the matrix of your DNA. If you feel balanced and integrated after those 7 times, then move on. If not, take some time to explore what may be causing you to feel uncentered by going deeper. Monitor your emotions, your thoughts and feelings in the physical body to determine if you are in resonance with each soundscape.

If the body shifts into a detox and purging process, then back off a bit until you feel it has cleared a layer of density. Use our Healing or Sanctuary CD during those times to assist in a more gentle way (see back of guide for more info). Of course, always do what feels right for you, less or more than 7 times. Everyone is going to be different with this, depending on where you are on your journey when you first started listening. Some people work with a soundscape for several months before moving on, so it is not something you need to rush through. Respect the process and don't push, as the results can cause you to backslide for a while until you can fully integrate the information. Assess your level of integration, how balanced and centered you determine yourself to be, not from your ego but from a heart centered place of honest self reflection.

> *Our intent is to unlock and activate the codex within the DNA through sound and vibration.*

If you have been meditating for some time and travel easily into other dimensional realms, but are not able to effectively actualize your higher visions and aspirations into your experienced reality, these soundscapes provide a tangible and supportive vibrational field in which a shift may occur. To make this connection easier to understand, you may consider one facet of what these soundscapes represent as being a kind of energetic food, or fuel. As many of you are aware, the quality of the physical food and the level of conscious intent with which it was prepared affect the health and wholeness of your physical structure, as well as your mental focus. You may choose organic vegetables over flesh based foods, because a vegetarian diet feels better, lighter and more full of Light on a higher octave. The level of clarity of the Body Temple affects the spectrum of your expression in matter. As you evolve to a more open, expanded and coherent state, you will naturally gravitate to that which supports your unfoldment. You will choose to follow your bliss over your lower self's addictive desires. The energetic "food" that we present to you on these CD's is, of course, not a replacement for physical nourishment. [unless you are from an alien culture that lives on plastic 😜]

The soundscapes will create a coherent, multidimensional wave of energy that harmonizes your environment, which you can ingest into your Light Body, your cellular memory and your DNA. When not meditating with them, we recommend just playing them quietly in the background of your living spaces. Listen to and absorb this field of energetic information into your structures as you breathe (prana) through your Chakra System, through Yoga/Qigong practices, through the alchemy of Ayurveda, through various higher vibrational essences and other supportive forms that are a part of the shapeshifting mandala of which you are now and are becoming.

The energy of the sonic information is absorbed through intent. Your belief and imagination are the conduit, the channel. The energy within the music is, in one sense a Tabula Rasa, a blank slate. It is a mirror that will reflect back what you believe you are and what you can be. The music does not impose anything upon you. It is based on the primal nature of the Universe, that of vibration, the basis of All That Is. The carrier wave of that vibration is Love, the love of wo/mankind and the unfolding planetary adventure that now lies before us. We will state that there are built in safeguards within the flow of the music that will not allow this energy to be utilized for dark purposes or by those beings who simply wish to push the envelope, through force of will, beyond a state of balanced growth. A natural state of repulsion will occur in these cases. If you are such a being, this will not be for you and you should seek elsewhere. With a state of open, trusting awareness, that which you desire will be revealed and seamlessly integrated into your life. The process of acceleration is one of consistency and perseverance, a daily devotional practice to become your full Light expressing in human form. Any aggressive actions to speed this up often leads to imbalances in your manifestations and ultimately frustrations that lead one to reject the validity of the process to quickly move on to the next thing — all valuable lessons ultimately. If you should decide to put them aside because you have determined them to not have value at this time, consider revisiting them every 6 months or so to see if that initial perception has shifted. With time comes wisdom.

This LevelOne Series was created to both ground your energy to the earth plane (3D) and expand your energy field to be able to easily shift your consciousness into the 4D/5D realms with full intention and fluidity. [NOTE: Some additional reading in the quantum physics field is suggested.] If either state, that of grounding or expanding, is dominant, an imbalance occurs and the activation process of your 12-strand DNA is slowed until you learn how to integrate all the frequencies. As you start activating these new strands of DNA on the etheric levels of your being, it is important to maintain a balanced flow of energy throughout the process. When you reach certain stages of this adventure, it will be impossible for you to move further until you assimilate the new energy more fully — it is not something that should be rushed, as we have already stated.

> *The dynamics of growth, renewal, evolution and structural differentiation are all functions and potentials of the organization of biophotonic field interactions.*

When we speak of balance, we mean that you have given considerable attention to each area in your life and that one area is not overly dominant. The areas are physical, emotional, mental and spiritual. In the physical area, this means you have a deeper understanding of the workings of the body, care for it and love it by exercising moderately, feeding it healthy, enlivening foods, cleanse and detox regularly and feel grounded and connected to it in a loving way. The emotional body requires inner reflection to understand the various feelings that arise. This will include various types of psychotherapy, emotional release work, inner child explorations and a control of emotional states from expressing extremes. The mental body requires the development of knowledge and qualities of analysis, discernment, rational thinking and thought management. The spiritual body expands to higher thoughts and wisdom beyond the affairs of the 3rd dimension. It needs deepened states of silence and meditation for contemplation and reflection throughout ones life. It needs a connection to something grander than the physical world. Create a pie chart for yourself and take a serious look back at your life and determine what your current state of balance is with all these states. If you find that there is an area that you are over emphasizing and one you are not paying so much attention to, then make the necessary adjustments. If any one of these dominate all others, you will be developing yourself in an unbalanced way and at some point, you will be stopped or slowed down significantly. Observe your days or weeks and determine how much time you are giving to each area of your life over a course of time and make the necessary adjustments.

As you raise your vibrational patterns and shift your areas of balance, the music will change and you will hear new sounds reflected back at you from different facets and curves of your experience of time and space. This will be a reflection of the work you are doing to attain balanced states. You will experience different feeling tones and shades of meaning that you did not hear or sense before. The multidimensional sounds are resonating the remembrance of who you are, continuing to evolve as you do. We have been listening to these sounds for almost 20 years and we still hear new patterns emerge. Thus far, they seem to have an almost endless reach of sonic landscapes for you to traverse. We attribute much of this to the expanding reach of our clairaudient abilities.

Paradoxically, although the music is a kind of multidimensional snapshot of a certain

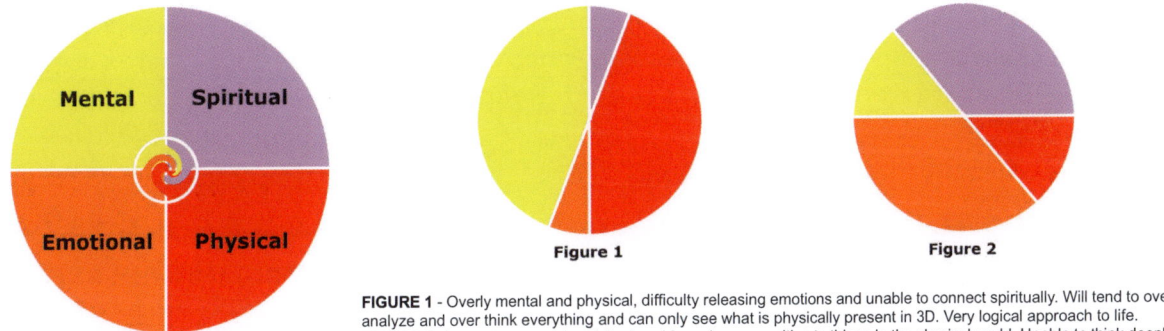

FIGURE 1 - Overly mental and physical, difficulty releasing emotions and unable to connect spiritually. Will tend to over analyze and over think everything and can only see what is physically present in 3D. Very logical approach to life.
FIGURE 2 - Loves to escape in spiritual worlds and very sensitive to things in the physical world. Unable to think deeply and ground higher visions into 3D. Very flighty and has lofty, fluffy presence with others.

energy field or state, it is also a living thing, a dynamic field of higher intelligence and information. That is the magic of what these soundscapes are, something that you will realize as you let go and go deeper. Worlds within worlds, doors and pathways to other dimensions are within them, reflections of that within you. The farthest spiraling out to the deepest within. It is simply a matter of perspective and directed intent. Remember, the quality and nature of the results experienced are in direct relationship to how you choose to interface with and interpret the material.

Building & Expanding Frequency Range

Each soundscapes builds upon the preceding one, which is why it is initially important to work with each one for a while before moving one. We will utilize the analogy of a scale with a 0 base line at the center point, ranging from +100 to −100 (frequency bands) on each side to illustrate this concept. If CD #1 ranges from +25 to −25, then each successive CD adds 25 in each direction (see Figure 3). Once a person has worked with all 4 CDs, they will have access to the full range of +/−100. On the −100 range, we could equate this to thoughts, feelings, emotions and experiences in the negative realms of human experience, while on the +100 range, we would experience the same in the positive realms. Example:

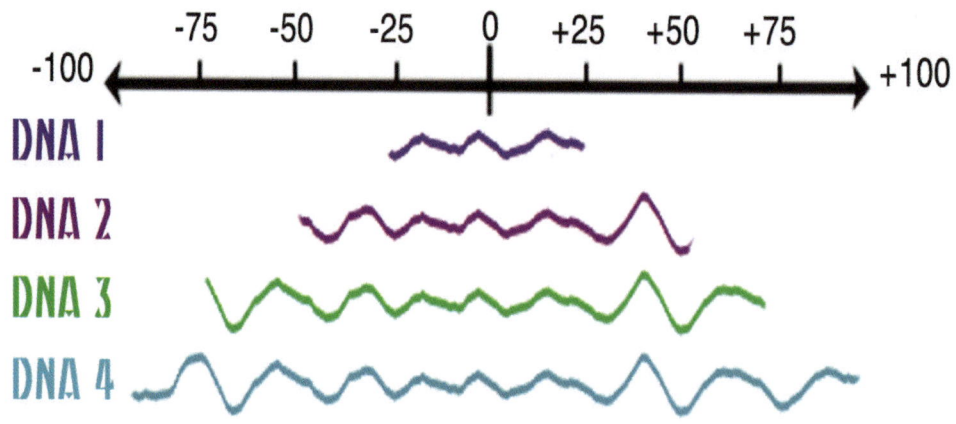

FIGURE 3

anger, hate, fear-based experiences vs. love, compassion, joy-based experiences (see Figure 4). Each CD is not limited to just its specified range either, each contains elements of each other superimposed over it which gives it the full multidimensional range of possibilities

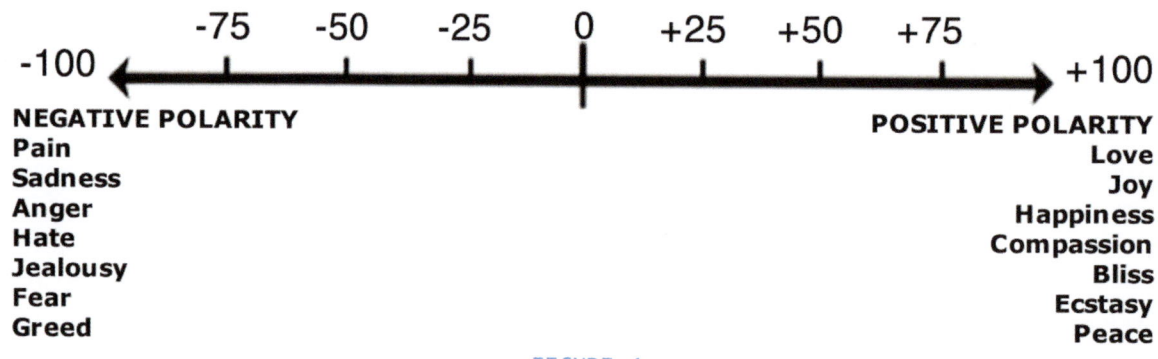

FIGURE 4

(see Figure 5). So even when listening to #1, a part of yourself is receiving frequencies from #2, #3 and #4. This allows you to gradually work towards a slow, steady integration process of all the frequency bands available in the LevelOne series initiation. Once you complete the first pass through all 4 soundscapes, you will then start moving up in a continual spiral of increasingly higher frequencies. You should maintain a balanced program by listening to them all as opposed to focusing on just one CD. At times you may work with one more than another, but be sure to also balance that out over time.

We trust that you understand the necessity to deal with the darker, denser aspects

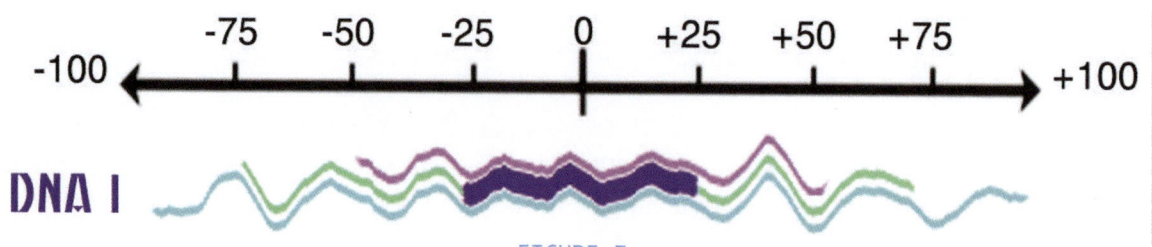

FIGURE 5

of being in human form in order to fully integrate who you are. This is a primary step in the initial activation process, one that you will move past eventually. By dipping into the heaviness of who you are and infusing it with Light, you have the opportunity to transmute this energy. You cannot know the full Light of your infinite potential without knowing the constricted Darkness of who you are. Like the swing of a pendulum, as you travel easily into the + range, you will then return with the swing of the pendulum back into the – range to clear any fear based energy blockages accreted from incarnational experiences. This is an on-going process throughout this LevelOne series that constantly spirals up, gradually lessening the extended visits in the darker realms.

As we evolve and begin to understand the cycles and rhythms of this evolving spiral, we no longer view the shadow realms of the Self as a bad thing, but something that we must transmute and transform to eventually lead our consciousness into greater states of bliss and joy. If you can learn to shift your perception of this space and release the excess baggage that it contains from lifetimes of similar energetic experiences, then you will be able to move much more quickly on to the more joy-filled states of being. There is tremendous power being stored/held in our shadow self that can be tapped as a source for greater energy enhancement, holding this belief allows you to see these experiences from a higher perspective. What could be called a state of enlightenment is attained when one achieves balance and transcends the full +/– range, as opposed to just seeking explorations into the +100 range. When you are ready to move out of that stage of the evolutionary process, you will then move on to the DNA LevelTwo soundscapes (see back of guide). You will know this by the higher states of Light being reflected in your 3D reality, which includes all your interactions and engagements.

LevelOne DNA Activation

We don't necessarily like to separate things by creating levels, however it is the best way for us to describe what is happening in this first series of soundscapes. As we evolve as a species, we gradually increase our Light Quotient to be able to exist within the more rarefied dimensional realms of reality. We currently have 2-strand DNA manifesting in our 3D level of reality, the additional 10+ strands or dimensional states that we are working towards activating, exist as interpenetrating overlays in the more subtle energetic realms of vibration and frequency. This LevelOne series lays the ground work and prepares the foundation to allow one to move into these more rarefied realms of Light while still maintaining the connection to the physical 3D reality. We feel it is equally important to actualize, balance and ground your manifestations in 3D before one can fully achieve resonance in more expanded levels of consciousness and realization.

Our base line potentials are being re-woven, re-connected, re-activated through stimulation from the galactic core.

The planetary shifts are accelerating and will continue to do so with or without your active participation. We are simply giving you tools that you may choose to utilize to raise your vibrational level to be in alignment with the evolutionary current, rather than being burned out, swept away by it or feeling continually out of sync with the world around you. These 4 soundscapes are building the multidimensional frequency maps to allow you to begin to gracefully explore these spaces; creating a smoother transition process. We are dropping the energetic sonic breadcrumbs as we continue to expand our consciousness further and further. Even though many of you have been doing personal/spiritual growth for years and even lifetimes, there are still experiential gaps within each of you that need to be harmonized in order to fully attain balance through the entire range of +/–100, as referred to in the previous section. These soundscapes will illuminate these frequency bands for you so that you can work on the appropriate areas of your life in order to come to a balanced state of consciousness. For some this may be dietary changes, release work, emotional clearing, exercise, more meditation or discipline in your spiritual practices, etc. — it will be different for each.

At this time we do not know how many levels of "The Work" will be created. We just recently completed the L2 series. We initiated our process of preparation for this series in 6/06 and started bringing through the soundscapes in 6/08. There are 6 soundscapes in this series. The DNA L2 frequencies will easily support you through the 2012-2023 timeline, enabling you to continually adjust to the higher frequencies as they pour on to the planet in waves. See back of guide for more info on this program.

All languages emerged from transmissions from the DNA itself to further direct wo/mankind's evolution at certain points on the timestream.

We imagine that we will continue to create new levels as we integrate each successive level, as well as that of the group energy that is supporting these frequencies to ground to the Earth grid. It is also possible that should we decide to transcend this realm one day, that we will have selected a successor to continue the work with our support on the higher realms. There really is no known plan at this time, as we continue to walk the journey, enjoying the unfolding process day by day.

Unfolding Teachings from a Sonic Mystery School

If an individual consciously, with loving intent, works with the 4 LevelOne soundscapes over an extended period of time and comes to a place where they can maintain an aware state at higher and higher levels in their meditation practices and shamanic journey work, the soundscapes will continue to unfold their teachings for many years. Your listening patterns will shift and change continually. You may feel an affinity to a specific soundscape for a period of time over all the others. It is recommended that you work with that one, but to not forgo one that you may decide you do not "like" as much or that it causes you to feel uncomfortable. It will be that soundscape that you should explore more deeply as your intent is to work through your stuck, rigid or blocked patterns in order to free up your energy for more expanded explorations. If a particular soundscape causes you unrest or discomfort, it is important that you continue to experience that energetic dynamic in the music and be aware of the issues that it is trying to bring to Light for you. As you do this, over time, it will transform what you might call darkness into the divine mystery of the magical realms of Light. With that said, if you are experiencing extreme imbalances in any area of your life, you should back off a while and use one of the more gentle soundscapes in our catalog, like Healing or Sanctuary (see back of guide). Once you find the Light even in the most challenging sonic passages, you will have accreted/assimilated a new level of expansiveness into your bio-energetic matrix. From that more open state you will know it is then time to move on to another soundscape and when you return to the previous one that may have caused some discomfort, you will notice something has significantly changed for you in the music. They will continue to shift and change as you evolve, as your Light Quotient increases, you will tune into different passages and frequencies that you did not pay attention to before.

The DNA is a receiver and a transmitter.

The first level integration can take anywhere from 4 months to many years depending on the individual's dedication, usage and directed intent; as well as their prior spiritual growth work before they started working with these transmissions. For many, this will also include a certain level of mental understanding of this material and so reading and attending various lectures/workshops will also facilitate a greater depth and appreciation of what is occurring. Even after several years of listening, they will continue to surprise you with something new.

These soundscapes are an initiatory process designed to shift the receptive listener's vibration into a resonant alignment with the advanced frequencies now occurring as we move into the next dimensional spiral of our collective existence. They will consistently align you with the 2012 frequencies, so that your life can maintain balance and flow in all areas. These soundscapes express an expansive sonic matrix to allow you to do this at your own pace. The boundaries within them are only set up by your inability to move past them. However, as you engage more and more, these boundaries will dissolve and a new level of the mystery unfolds. We believe that one's own higher guidance will indicate when it is time to move on to the next level or the next set of frequencies.

You will experience initiations in the higher realms that will be made aware to you through dreams and visions that indicate a new level has been attained. From time to time, you may want to stop listening for a while to integrate the increase of Light and awareness into your daily lives. Take time out to listen to nature and engage with other musical adventures. When you return again, a whole new level of experience will emerge. We also highly recommend that you work with the other soundscapes in our catalog as each of them will hold a specific focus within it that is only basically represented in the DNA Series. It is like the DNA Series is the sonic encyclopedia and the other soundscapes are separate books taken out and expanded upon. See our description of these soundscapes in the back of this guide.

We are not suggesting that you only listen to these soundscapes to the exclusion of all other music that you enjoy. Only that you dip into the wellspring of our offering often to continue to increase and unfold the blissful potential of your becoming. We will gently suggest that along with enjoying the energetic banquet of sound now available to you on the planet, that you continue to snack on our nutritional and transformational frequencies that will provide you with much more than your minimum daily requirements of Light☺. We have found that those who really GET the full scope and potency of these soundscapes listen to them on a daily basis, even if just throughout the night as they sleep or in the background of their environments. Listening deeply at least a few times a week will provide you with enough energetic support to maintain a consistent higher state of flow in you life.

Truth Emerging within Sound

Throughout our development, we have remained very eclectic in our approach to walking the spiritual path. This allows us to freely tap into all sources of potential truth contained within teachings that we consider to be in alignment with The Light or The Source of All That Is. This allows you, the listeners, to connect with your own channel of information without being influenced by what we may call truth. Example: if you are Buddhist, Christian, Jewish, Native American, African, Hindu, Taoist, Toltec, Muslim, a creative channel of the New Edge, if you connect with Nature, Magick, Alchemy, the Quabbalah, the Creative Muse of the Arts, or if you come from Andromeda, Pleaidies, Sirius, Eros, Venus or Mars, etc. you will find that a deepening of your current of information is contained within these soundscapes. All paths lead to The One. As Dorothy did in the Wizard of Oz, all you have to do is follow the yellow brick road, getting off and on again, only to find out in the end that what you seek was inside you all of the time — inside your DNA, a place called HOME.

Going back to what we said about the multidimensional way in which this music is composed — it is not limited to

> *One might conclude that human languages are a reflection of the patterns within the DNA codex.*

any one thoughtform or belief system. It is emanating from The Source which contains all beliefs in support of Love. We encourage you to follow your current inclinations and use the techniques that you feel most comfortable with while exploring these soundscapes. Be open to exploring new and more expanded realms of knowledge as you work with these soundscapes, as they will challenge you to look deeper in what you currently believe to be your reality. Review our Listening Suggestions chapter for many ideas on how to expand upon and deepen your explorations with these soundscapes.

In addition to the above statements, there are several sources of information with various approaches, who are traveling around the planet teaching specific classes in DNA Activation techniques. If you have the opportunity to take one of these workshops, we suggest that you consider doing so. Choose the resource that feels right for you. You will come to a deeper understanding of how consciously working with the DNA can assist your process of evolution. Each of these teachers also have available either books or tapes that you may acquire to expand your knowledge about DNA healing techniques. We offer links to teachers and books on our website.

You may also decide that you want a vibrational healer to initiate the process of activating your DNA. This is very much like Shaktipat, passing on of energy that can help you to lift your Light level past what you can normally achieve on your own. Because they have been doing the work for sometime, they basically are giving you a Step Up in the process. It is important that you feel resonance with this person before you allow them to do DNA Activation on you. We also offer this service as well as other spiritual readings that will help you to understand where you are on your journey. Sometimes it is a good idea to do some preliminary work before diving into the activation process. Review our spiritual guidance information on The 3rd Eye in the back of this guide.

Ultimately we want you to find your own truths, to engage with this process and find out where you really are empowered to share your Light. Our beliefs are irrelevant to the process and we are not here to impart them upon you. We will share our current path with you at anytime you would like to communicate with us, but we ask that you remember that it is our journey and you need to discover you own. We are about empowering each of you to find your full creative expression and to share that unique gift with the world. We believe with all our experience on this journey that these soundscapes are a very powerful tool that can assist you greatly in the process.

Blending with other Programs and Techniques

The DNA Activation soundscapes will enhance any process that you are currently working on and provide you with a range of frequencies that will enable you to receive your own guidance on the directions you need to take in order to actualize your full potential. Depending on one's frame of reference and approach to this work, you can use the music to follow that path or find a new one as you are guided. You will find places of resonance with any other path of Light within these soundscapes. The music is not imposing any teachings upon you, it is allow you to find where your heart is and to expand and grow that Light within you directed by your sincere intentions.

The music creates a coherent, multidimensional wave of energy that harmonizes your environment, which you can ingest into your Light Body, your cellular memory and your DNA.

This music is channeled from a place of pure intent and for the aware listener it can be a multi-dimensional resource of evolutionary knowledge and wisdom. Over time, one can learn how to tap into certain frequency bands that contain information you seek and bring sonic transmissions back into the 3D level of reality in the form of thoughts, words, language or artistic interpretations (see Figure 6). These frequency bands can contain volumes of information on specific teachings that you are engaged with or seek

DNA Activation/Shapeshifter

to learn more about, especially those that have a large body of work accumulated within them. As an example, Christianity, Buddhism, Taoism, Hinduism, Mystery Schools, etc. Even beyond these more earth-based teachings, there are more cosmic teachings available as one learns how to expand their consciousness into the omni-dimensional Universe. It is a stepping down through the frequency bands that occur with this process. First it feels like energy movement, blissful sensations in the body, then in the days/weeks to follow, you will start hearing new thoughts and ideas being released in your mind. Visions will come through your third eye and in your dreams that will further help you unfold the information. These transmissions do have to move through several filters of belief and are also affected by the level of clarity, emotional balance and physical health/vitality of the listener before they actually translate into the linear written or spoken word. Because of these factors, some of the essence of the transmission can be lost in processing. By stating your intention prior to connecting with certain vibrational patterns, you establish a connection to that particular source of information. You can either allow yourself to remain in a state of silence and let that frequency harmonize within your vibrational essence or you can attempt to create language/communication/art from the transmission. Artistic expressions can flow more easily as it bypasses the mental processing needed for words to come forth to explain or analyze.

It is with clarity and resolve that we travel into these realms of infinite possibilities, acting as an open channel to bring through these higher dimensional frequencies to Modulate the Lifewave. As our life path is focused on the process of DNA Activation, the listener is invited to resonate with and "surf upon" the waves of sound to assimilate vistas of experience beyond the limitations of logical thought. As you do this process more and more, you will gain a greater understanding of the work that we are doing to bring these soundscapes through, as you will do the same with your particular form of creative expression.

Many are bringing

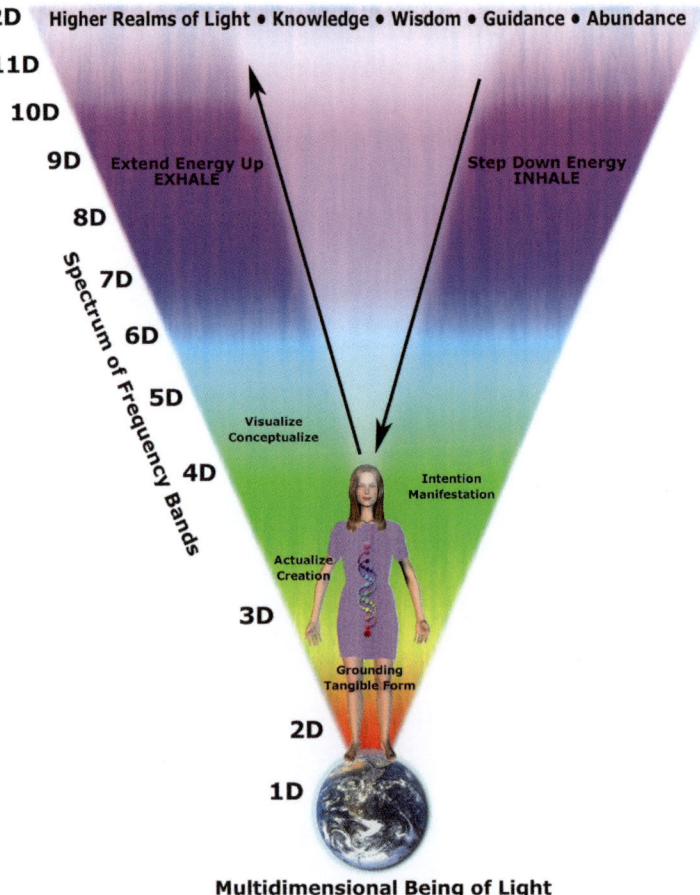

FIGURE 6. Engaging in process of co-creation with the Universal Energy Field.

through information today about how to activate the DNA and they all have various parts of the puzzle to offer. We do not mean to take anything away from any of the current teachers of this knowledge, as we really have not studied their works because we have our own path to follow. They are bringing through some very valuable information that enables the seekers of this knowledge to understand some of the steps that are important in awakening the process of DNA Activation within the human bio-energetic matrix. We encourage you to explore the various aspects of this information available as you feel guided. As with any form of channeling or teachings of higher wisdom, the quality and purity of information being received is dependent on the person's ability to maintain a connection with these higher vibrational states of consciousness, while walking a dedicated path of Light. Our path is to offer these sonic frequency maps for all to establish these connections, maintain them and integrate them into their energetic field, gradually building their body of Light. Because our work is non-linear and multidimensional, we feel it compliments any of the other teachings you might be working with.

> *Certain resonant frequencies have profound effects on the codes within the DNA, keys that have been waiting for thousands, perhaps millions of years for the right evolutionary sequence to be activated.*

The music will become a trusted friend and a wise counsel for you for many, many years. This relationship is like any others that you have, it takes time to let it develop. It is not a one-time transmission or a workshop/training that is over in a weekend. You will be able to work with these every day or whenever you feel you need support as you continue to walk this journey of unfolding your potential. They will always be there waiting for you.

Active vs. Passive Listening

There are 2 primary ways to play these soundscapes — passively in the background or actively while deeply engaged. For optimal effectiveness and consistent results, you should "work" with them daily or at least 3-4 times per week. Working with them is different from passively listening. To work with them, you should listen on a high quality stereo system with a sub-woofer and good set of external speakers. The better the high and low range of your sound system the more expansive the experience will be. Use what you currently have available and consider upgrading your system as you increase your understanding of the power of sound in your life. Every player you play them on will also produce a different result. The volume should be louder than background music, but lower than dance music. You want to FEEL the music throughout your body as you are listening. If you do not currently own a full range stereo system, find a friend who does just for the experience. Also if you can find someone in your area with a sound table, be sure to explore them there as well.

You will expand your awareness of the sounds, gradually deepening your experience by becoming the music and allowing it to play you. You will slip in and out of being aware of your physical body by learning how to sense and feel the world around you from an energetic perspective. The AYD #2 DVD Training Program has a series of techniques to help you develop these skills (see back of guide). The more you learn how to connect with your energy body and allow it to become more fluid and flowing with the music, the more you will start to become aware of how it is affecting your life in the same way (see Figure 7). As you add your intentions to this process and actually start working with the energy all around you to manifest and actualize your dreams and desires, you will come to know how powerful the music is in assisting you in this process. It is by engaging consciously with the soundscapes, that you will start to see a world full of magic and wonder appearing before you eyes. Synchronicities and miracles of all kinds emerge as these are the doorways

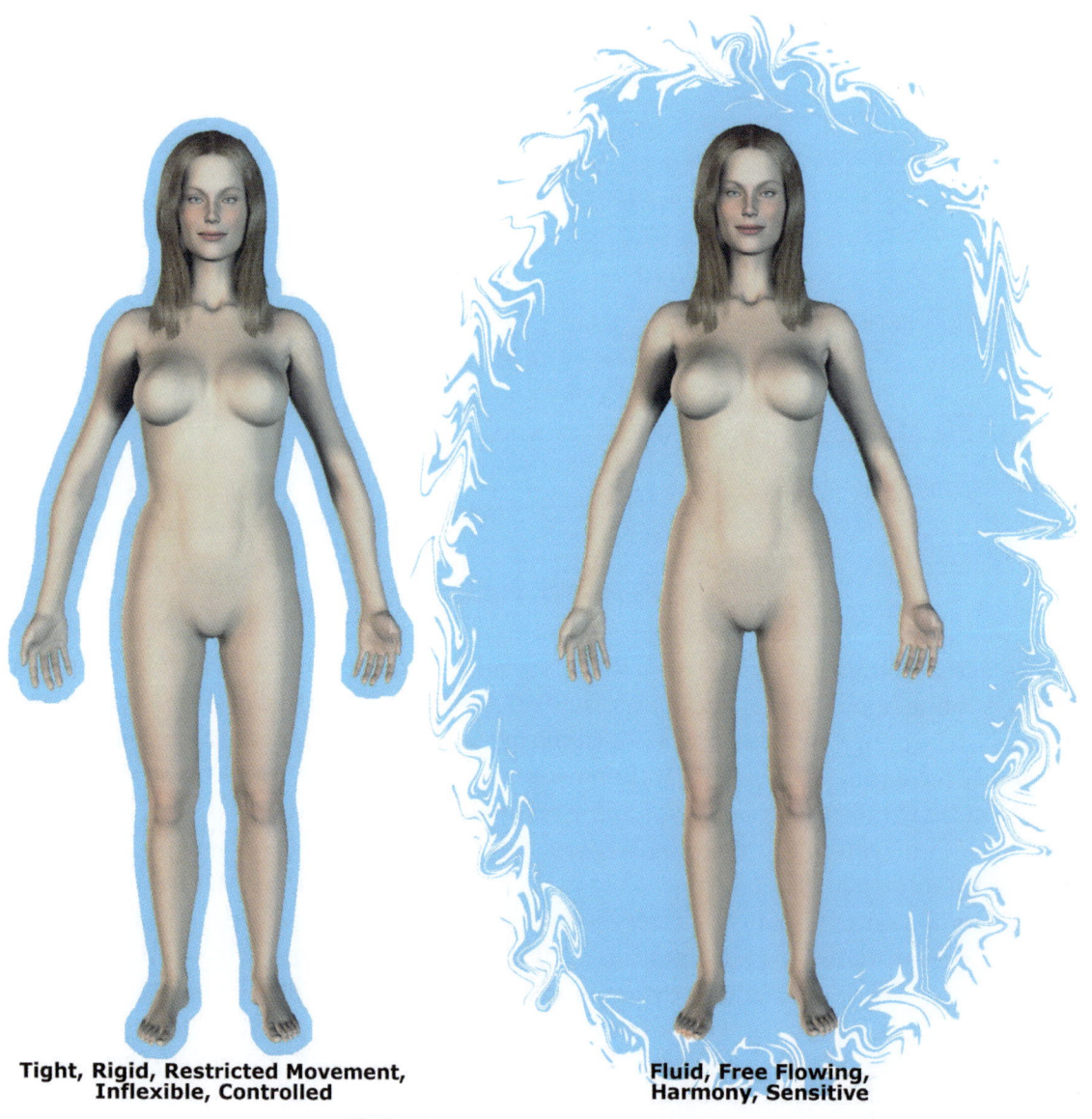

Tight, Rigid, Restricted Movement, Inflexible, Controlled

Fluid, Free Flowing, Harmony, Sensitive

FIGURE 7. Energy body superimosed over physical body.

into the 5th World manifestations. Because the music is harmonically connected to these multidimensional realms via an organic state of higher flows, it allows you to easily move into these spaces of heightened potentials.

It is also a good idea to play these soundscapes in the background of your environments as they will keep the vibrational fields around your home/office/car at consistently higher levels of Light — ultimately creating a very powerful vortex of energy that will assist you in all your manifestation processes as you move about the World. If you are not a well-grounded person and not used to working and functioning in 3D in higher states of consciousness, then we recommend that you do not play them while driving until such time as you honestly feel you have integrated the energy more fully.

We also recommend playing them quietly throughout the night while you sleep as they will assist you in your multidimensional travels and lucid dreaming states. As you shift in and out of consciousness during the night, the sounds will provide energetic support and a sanctuary for you in your nocturnal adventures in very interesting and wonderful ways. You can program yourself to tune into the sounds and let them guide you in your dreaming states.

Prior to going to sleep and upon arising are very key times to tune into the sounds and work with them for optimal results in your manifestations. Move into deep meditative states for longer and longer periods of time, gradually decreasing your sleep time and expanding this semi-awakened state for several hours at a time. This is the place where the most profound connections can be made to your higher guidance and clairvoyant visions can be the strongest. This is considered theta and delta states of consciousness.

Evolution, by its very nature, is not always what you expect.

You can also listen to these soundscapes with headphones from time to time. While it is not the primary listening tool, it is one that should be explored to further assist in moving into higher states of whole brain functioning. You will find yet again, a whole new spectrum of musical sounds to explore using your headphones.

Your interactions with the music can become private therapy, counselling and coaching sessions for you as well. You can share your life and ask questions and receive guidance back in the form of imagery, symbols or words of wisdom. When done daily, deeper insights into your life path are continuously revealed allowing you to move forward much more quickly with manifesting your dreams and desires. You don't end up getting stuck in as many of the dramas that can be played out for long durations, which ultimately drain your life force and weaken your desires. Being able to catch things quicker before they manifest into dramatic situations is a very powerful gift of insight.

As for effecting others around you who may be living in your space, you may want to tell them about the music or not, it is up to you to decide if you feel they would understand or want to know. You will not be harming them in any way as their internal evolutionary directives can only be activated by their conscious intent and directed will. Some people may not enjoy the soundscapes as it is just not their time to begin to shift into these vibrational realms. The sounds in the CDs may be too strange or odd to their hearing. In this case, just honor their space and do not play them when they are around. Others will be very attracted to them, not knowing why at first. They will ask you to tell them more about them or you will start noticing changes in their behavior and attitudes. If you are playing them for your family in the hopes that they will awaken, it is entirely possible that they will clearly be affected, if they are ready. You will also notice children, pets and plants responding in wonderful and unusual ways.

Expanding your Consciousness

It is probable that at times spontaneous out of body experiences (OBE), as well as other similar phenomena, will occur as you go deeper into becoming the sound. You are learning how to unstick the energy body from the physical as you do this. The more intentionally you work with the music, the more likely this effect is going to occur. You may also spontaneously raise the kundalini energy as well, so just be aware of what this is and what may occur.

Some level of discernment should be obtained prior to engaging consciously to generate an OBE. Be honest with yourself, go within and access your state of physical vitality, health and mental equilibrium before committing to a prolonged series of these types of explorations. If you are in an unbalanced emotional state, you may further weaken your energy as out of body travels draw upon the physical vehicle's reserve of Life Force to project "outward." You must strengthen and balance your body temple and utilize appropriate methods to replenish your chi force or you could create an imbalance.

You should also be proficient in core level protection of your spiritual/emotional field to shield yourself from undesirable influences. We find that many people are fascinated with spiritual phenomena and this is all part of learning how to claim the power within you that has always been there. If having an OBE or raising your kundalini gives you validation that you are in fact evolving, then by all means go ahead and explore it from this perspective, with the proper precautions as stated above. In addition to the OBE, you can also consider remote viewing, time travel, levitation, telepathy, shapeshifting, transmutation and teleportation skills; which all require similar training and developmental skills. The AYD #2 DVD (see back of guide) will help you to prepare for this work and offers some excellent beginning exerices for loosening up the energy body for greater flexibility. To assist you in this process, we recommend that you have already acquired some knowledge about this subject and have some techniques that you are working with. You can use the soundscapes to travel on with your consciousness and the more you let go into the sound patterns and Become the Music, the more you will be able to let go of "being in the body." Sound is a powerful way to practice OBEs, because it provides you with a frequency map from which you can extend your consciousness outward using the patterns of sound and then travel back on these modulations into your physical body. For beginners, it is good practice to expand your consciousness out through the crown chakra as far as you can go

> *Consider one facet of what these CD's represent as being a kind of energetic food, or fuel.*
> *The energy of the music is absorbed through intent.*

while holding an aware state of consciousness and then enter back through the crown, going through the body and then out the root chakra into the earth. If you work with this for a while, expanding and contracting gradually, eventually you will experience the feelings of being out of body when you travel. It is a matter of learning how to "let go."

In our personal approach to conscious explorations into various realms, we often travel inward. It can actually be experienced as one and the same reality, sort of a turning inside out using worm holes/time displacement portals to shift to other realities. Deeper studies on these subjects are recommended.

The chakra system, in this sense, can be conceived as a series of interlinked, interdimensional spiraling vortexes to other profound energetic states. All that you seek is within the stored information in the DNA. The DNA is also a spiraling vortex, a miniature wormhole. When we travel inward, we invoke, with intent, the energy of integration and the coming together of all dimensions of experience within the Body Temple, the soul's vehicle while incarnate in the physical. When you come to the realization that matter is as spiritual as any other level of existence, you will begin to glimpse a more expansive paradigm and a new way of being.

Consider the possibility that the real reason we are here is not simply to reincarnate throughout many lifetimes learning lessons of love, consciousness and interaction along the way. We, as a race, have been stuck in that co-dependent loop, within our belief of that worldview extending over eons of time. Try to understand that we, as a species, may very well be playing that game of life, death and rebirth because our attention and intent has been entrained to do so. It's just the way it is mentality. One of our real purposes for being "here" may be to achieve multidimensional awareness in matter, within any given state, to transcend the limitations of the form. Not to artificially inflate the lower ego, but to become joyous co-creators guided by and in harmony with

> *Whether the energetic metaphor is 12, thousands or an unfolding number of strands: approaching infinity consider that the grounding of the work begins in the two.*

the Isness of the All. In this way, growth and the unfolding process further adds to the sum total of experience and the Whole becomes, within the wondrous play of The Game, much more than the sum of its parts.

12 Strands and Beyond

Before reading this section, begin by expressing gratefulness to the Universe for the profound wonder of your existence and experience. Our word pictures contain deeper harmonics and currents of the highest intent. These transmissions were captured from the current of information generated from our interaction with the DNA soundscapes — listening to the music in a deeply focused and aware state while in the process of writing. These word affirmations are in a flow, rhythm, rhyme and timing to open up your paradigms. By listening to the music while reading this guide, they will provide a sanctuary, a profound vibrational space in which you can explore the concepts we share with you. You will find that your consciousness will flow on the waves of sound and being in this flow will also help you to visualize, opening your neural pathways and kinesthetic senses to deeper levels of information. Our soundscapes oscillate through all spectrums of manifestation, from the two strands through the etheric harmonic overlays (10+ dimensional states) that some have semantically termed the other strands.

Much has been said about activating these other 10 "strands" of DNA and about the energetic seals placed upon them to keep humankind from reaching the full potential of 12 strand actualization. Some sources now speak of 22 strands or even thousands of strands as yet to be activated. Whether the energetic metaphor is 12, thousands or an unfolding number of "strands" approaching infinity, consider that the grounding of the work begins in the two. These DNA soundscapes assist the energetic blocks/seals/frequency fences to dissolve and allows the living information to reintegrate and re-link with the 2 strands now tangibly present in 3D. For the purposes of this exploration, it does not matter how or why these separating seals were placed there, only that they can now be removed — What was Hidden, is now Revealed.

You do not need to be a mechanic to drive a car. We are simply giving you one view of what is under the hood, so to speak. We are showing you these things to spark your remembrances to unlock the doors of your akashic records. Within your current memory matrix, you have codes that are set to open when you reach a certain vibratory state. The music is the sonic key that unlocks these inner secrets. Rather than give you dry mazes of explanations that lead to more mental masturbation and self referential closed loop gratification within your imagination, we are giving you a multi-level experience. Listen to the music and read the words. Use the synergy to expand your awareness so that the transmission will anchor on a deeper level.

All of these visualizations, shapes and levels are simply tools. The map is not the territory — always remember this. Use your imaginative faculties to invoke the images of the DNA that feel right for you. Center yourself, go within and speak to your DNA as if you were speaking to a wise and loving friend. You will then be communicating directly with your DNA in a way that feels right for you, to the "heart of the matter." You can then put a familiar face upon the essence, beyond the form and bridge with this loving energy in your personal sanctuary. As you begin to activate and re-connect the pathways, the conduits that connect the dots restructure the connecting matrix within the dormant codes. These connecting vortexes, reflected at increasing levels of "density" through the harmonics of manifestation, form the hologram of All That Is.

It is time to embrace your feeling nature, for Love is the higher communion between the molecules of emotion, activating your body of Light and allowing you to reclaim your heritage on an evolving earth and with your interdimensional/intergalactic origins. Your intent, will direct this experience. The path of higher evolution is to ask to be shown the more expansive aspects of your being and your connection to the collective consciousness of the planet and All That Is.

To assist you in integrating this knowledge on deeper levels, we will add the following experiential exercise for you to incorporate while reading this information:

Start by relaxing and inhaling/exhaling deeply. Continue breathing from your center and allow your heart chakra to unfold like an expanding flower throughout this process. Remain aware. Visualize a sparkling current of Light entering your body through not only the nose and mouth, but through the crown chakra at the top of your head and from the ground through the central pillar of your spine. The luminous egg that is your energetic field glows ever brighter, as the energy begins to pulsate through your field transmuting those areas within your physical vehicle that feel blocked or constricted. Visualize this energy, the energy of Love, lighting up the energetic field that is you. Maintain conscious awareness as the energy spirals, first one direction and then perhaps the other, through your field, seeking its own true pathways of connection. Now take this energy in through the surface of the skin, through every pore, cleansing, renewing, healing, refining and transforming. Your inner beauty now merges and becomes manifest in your outward appearance as your structure begins to glow from within. Allow the energy to naturally gravitate to any areas of tension that you are holding within the body structure. Allow those areas of cellular memory to speak to you, through feelings, impressions and images. Allow whatever is appropriate from this inner dialogue to rise to the surface of your awareness without examination or judgment. Let these images dissolve and transform into the Light. Waves of bliss and joy begin coursing through your body as your cells awaken to a new level of functioning, as the energetic matrix of your body temple begins to assume a new way of being. Go deeper, while keeping your intent lightly focused.

Feel this energy of Love, of Universal Oneness, the nectar of the gods in your tissues, muscles, organs, bones and cells. You are the Alchemy, you are the Soma, you are the Philosopher's Stone — awaken to your true divinity. Synapses are connecting in novel ways within your brain and your neural network. Go deeper. Your feeling/sensing nature is becoming more and more refined. Feel and allow the visualization to emerge, sense that the electron spin of the atoms of your physical being are expanding, taking a wider elliptical orbit. While still maintaining a grounded sense of self, you are becoming less dense, less contracted on all levels. You are becoming more fluid, more flowing, as you stretch the boundaries of what you believed you were, what you have been told you were, what you have convinced yourself through many incarnations that you are. Go deeper, into the dancing particle waves of the subatomic, to the energetic boundary that some scientists term dark matter (a better term is actually superluminal matter). At this juncture, zero point energy emanates from this energetic dimensional transition zone and coordinates of meaning emerge into the hologram of this harmonic universe, what has been termed the dimension of 3D.

Become One with All That Is

These coordinates or locations in time/space emerge from our known 3D vibrational matrix, which emanate from the conscious intent you set forth on many dimensional levels of your being. As these coordinate points shift in relationship to each other, different harmonics

DNA Activation/Shapeshifter

43

are formed and new possibilities become manifest. Various energy states are formed from the angle of interaction of these points of focus, what some scientists have called scalar fields. When we say points, angles, fields etc., we are simply giving you something that you can, as the saying goes, "wrap your head around." From these fields of potential, up from the dancing field of particle/waves, the 2 strand structure of DNA emanates, connecting to the superluminal and arising from it, a holographic vessel that acts as a receiver, a projector and a transmitter. Realize that the concept of levels is ultimately a semantic structure. When you believe you are going inward, you are also projecting outward. Because in truth, we have not as yet realized in a tangible manner, that we are connected to everything at once and communication within the superluminal transcends the so called limitations of the speed of light, space and time.

Within the vast unexplored landscape of the two strand DNA are the connecting points that interface with what geneticists have termed the "letters" — the nucleotide base pairs that form a repeating sequence series in an as yet unknown language. We submit that these sequences are a symbolic representation, a calling card if you will, that expresses a much deeper reality. In one ironic sense, one could say that they are the alien evolutionary barcodes of the many species of which our DNA is composed, the signature of our creators. You didn't realize that you had alien DNA within you! Wo/mankind, incarnated in our present form, is an artistic combination of on and off planet origins. There is no escaping this fact, so you may as well accept that. Embrace your heritage, for all is as it should be in the Divine Unfolding of All That Is. The human species contains bits of code from Pleiadian, Orion, Niburian, Sirian, Andromedan and many other species and races as well as Gaian home material. It is this unique mixture that makes us what we are. It is not really that hard to comprehend this as we have seen this mixing and blending of races on our own planet — just take it to another level — as above, so below and vice versa.

These codes are the energetic connections to the etheric overlays of the other qualities/dimensions that have been termed "strands." In other words, these etheric strands equate to dimensional states. They are not ultimately separate as you might visualize bands or strata of energy, but interpenetrate each other in a holistic synergy when re-integrated within the fully realized dual strand structure. Separation is an illusion created by the holographic imprint seals, previously mentioned, that were inserted into the DNA in the distant past of our shared reality to create this effect. It was actually a gift to allow us to integrate multidimensional reality at a pace in which the physical form could maintain stability without spontaneously combusting. Many of you are now at a sufficient level of consciousness and Light Quotient for the possibility to exist for the frequency fences to be dissolved and for re-integration to occur. You are in control of this process and you always have been. It has been your focus of attention that has prevented you from breaking through into these higher realms.

Go within and speak to your DNA as if you were speaking to a wise and loving friend.

A workable initial model has to do with the visualization of relationships, what can be termed coordinate points of energy, which are in essence, points of focused intent. You may visualize these connections within the codex as a transparent circuit board of shifting pathways, the lines of directed intent connecting the circuits as interpenetrating beams of light, like a glowing fiber optic display. Begin by conceptualizing a 2D flat plane surface of these lines connecting points of reference in this way. Now expand your awareness and watch as this surface becomes a cube in 3 dimensions. Allow your consciousness to go further. The structure will at some point begin to shapeshift, folding your perception of time and space. Let the form of these connections become whatever it wishes to become. You will then experience a symbolic display, of what has been termed sacred geometry. These symbols are a manifestation of what has been termed the Language of Light, which is capable of holding infinite depths and shades of meaning within these archetypes for you to discover. These symbols will morph into visions, into waves of feeling and emotion and into actual manifestations of wonder with your 3D experience. Wherever your attention is fixed, whatever dimensional realm you agree to hold predominant belief in, will be the reality you experience during your current life.

We are showing you one method that, if faithfully pursued, will lead you to the possibility of multidimensional enlightened awareness within the dream of your waking reality. You will learn how to hold the essence of the process even while doing what you may consider to be the most mundane tasks. In truth, all that you do can be a celebration of life, if you so choose. You will each receive the information that is uniquely matched to you, for you direct your communication towards that which is termed You, through the artistic expression of your current incarnation, that is your unfolding Present. You have now initiated contact with your DNA and can return to this experience at any time to deepen the communion and communication. The more you choose to joyfully embody and integrate these possibilities expressed in Love, the more you will transform and thus add to the unfoldment of a more expansive, uplifting probable future for all.

> *Within your current memory matrix, you have codes that are set to open when you reach a certain vibratory state. The music is the sonic key that unlocks these inner secrets...*

As you continue to do this process daily while listening to the DNA Activation CDs, as you read our words, as you eat your nourishment, or work, make love, exercise, meditate and live your life to the fullest; gently without force of will, as far as you can go each time, the more Light Quotient you will be able to accrete. Soon you will be able to invoke this process on command, with your intent, at any time. You are anchoring a profoundly expansive state into your being, be patient and gentle with yourself. Instead of feeling that time is speeding up, that there is little time left to change, you will realize that the Point of Power is in the Present, and that you have all the time in the world. Drop the pressure and dogma of supposed planetary activation timelines or quotas that need to be achieved by certain fixed dates. These are distractions to entrain you to a more limited, fear based scenario. Choose the wisdom of a higher path. You cannot effectively manifest while under the self imposed pressure of these deadlines or fear structures. No one definitively knows what the outcome will be. There are lots of postulations that are derived from an incomplete scope of knowledge. Knowledge on this level lacks the multidimensionality of the Infinite, so what you end up getting is snippets of partial truths. The most powerful truth to accept is to Relax into the Flow and Be. The future is in flux and what probable reality we experience is surely shaped by our collective intent. You will no longer slack, but will act and interact. But you will act and interact with life from a profoundly expanded, yet grounded center.

You are now consciously aligning with the waves of transcendent energy from the galactic core, through the magnetic/electromagnetic pulsing of our sun's energetic field, effecting the bioenergetic matrix of GAIA, the blue-green jewel that is your 3D home. You thrive in this energy and will grow, evolve and become the magic of what you truly are. You will, day by day, become a place holder for more and more joy, more feeling, more awareness and more Light. As you begin to live and embody your highest dreams and visions, bit by bit, day by day, others will resonate and each in their own way will do the same.

We choose not to name the sources of, or specifically relate to any one current of information we bring to you, whether from this planet, other dimensions or the stars — although many would have us speak specifically for them or align with their agendas. This is not our way. We are Shapeshifter, we are the renegades, artists, adventurers and explorers; shamans engaged with the journey directly. We choose to remain open, to fluidly move between states of being and between worlds. Come dance with us, friends, and share your dreams, your mysteries and your mythos. Come share, with us, the joy of being alive at this momentous time in history and choose to manifest your highest most expansive visions from the nexus of the unfolding Now.

A further unfolding of the rhyme on the back cover of DNA CD #3:

A BRIDGE LINKS GAIA, HUMAN, ALIEN, AND DIVINE
(the DNA)

A COMMON GROUND BEYOND SPACE AND TIME
(the Superluminal)

FOR IN TRUTH ALL EMERGED FROM SAME
(The shared codex)

DIFFERENT ASPECTS OF THE GAME
(Our shared artistic creations)

LINES OF PROBABILITY CONVERGE
(the scalar field matrixes)

PAST, PRESENT AND FUTURE MERGE
(formed by directed intent, no outcome is fixed)

IN THE POINT OF POWER
(Gratefulness, Faith, Love, Devotion to the Higher Good and Trust)

IN THE NEXUS OF THE NOW
(Your unfolding awareness)

SYNCHRONICITIES AND INFINITE PROBABILITIES EMERGE
(the more you reach out to It, the more It reaches back to you)

A Journey into the Lands of Science

If everything in this companion guide were simple, what fun would that be? With that said, this section of the book will be a little on the intellectual/heady side. Some of you reading this will find it fascinating to explore the potentials of the DNA soundscapes with these deeper word pictures, while others may get lost in the myriad labyrinth of concepts on the edge. It is good to stretch one's perceptions, beliefs and consciousness in order to keep the evolutionary processes moving along. Those who juggle intellectual paradigms may find it too soft, with not enough meat on the bone. Still, there's vital marrow in that bone and in the interface between these written words and the music. It's a gestalt and a synergy. We have endeavored to find a middle ground, between erudite pomposity and mushy simplicity to present these complex, interwoven concepts. At times, while writing this, we felt that we should be wearing a smoking jacket and puffing on the stereotypical tobacco pipe. Dictionaries are available in the lobby.

The music is the sacred, shining common ground of our work and our play. So listen to the CDs and read this section when and if you feel guided to do so. Come back again in time to explore it further and it will start to unfold for you the many multidimensional layers of reality.

**Scalar Field Dynamics =
field of information accessed by heartfelt feeling
that takes you ever deeper into Love.**

Here's a bit of playful humor to "lighten" things up before we delve into the heavier material. Everybody, sing along with our rap to a hip-hop beat, follow the dancing biophotonic ball.

> Put this info in the hopper, let it blend, let it converge. Let it merge. All the big words and concepts are just paradigms, which are shifting all the time, sense the essence, feel the presence, of the Light that shines. Beneath the syllables and the nouns, is a luminous common ground. The words are but fingers pointing to the moon or colorful balloons of hot air, floating upward into an endless expanse of sky, beyond the reasons and the whys. Be without a care, neither here nor there, let go of doubt and fear. We are all connected and protected, just realize that you are. Ever blending, never ending in the language of your becoming, within your cells and DNA, reality is what you focus your intent upon, so express within each moment, the highest and the best of that which you truly mean to say. Look behind the curtain, go on, take a peek. Reality shapeshifts to conform to your beliefs, becoming all ways that which you seek. Commune and communicate, be flexible and you'll move in the flow, there is always more than what you think you know. Through the hologram of living, each experiences the world through unique and sacred eyes, Realize — as you open up your feelings and keep believing you understand,

> I AM that I AM, the unfolding plan, you will embody all the Love you feel you can, and receive a thrill of recognition, that will spark your intuition. Embrace the paradox, and the masks will melt, the veils will drop, your hold on time will stop. You will not scatter, or disperse, or mutate into some alien curse. You will feel more real than you have ever felt before, as you travel through many paths and many doors, no need to keep score, of what you think is right or wrong, just bang the Gong and get it on, ground the energy, sing the song, make it up as you go along. Sing the body electric, overtone a new vibration, a new and righteous tune, be wild, and free, don't hold back, howl at the moon. Here's another clue, you know what to do. The more you reach out to IT, the more IT reaches back to you. Be honest, be sincere and true to that which moves you, in the colors that you fashion, from the burning fire of your passion. You dance the dance in graceful remembrance of who you are, for every man and every woman is a Star. Starseed you are, your origin and heritage, beyond death and beyond age. As the tapestry of the 12 is rewoven, the illusion of the controllers broken and dissolved in Love, not rage. In the dawning, a new blending — of scientist, artist, shaman, philosopher and sage.

The following information is a blending of quotes and references from frontier science, intuitive insights and channeled information we have received. Any material quoted does not imply the sources quoted in any way endorse our interpretation of their material. In fact, spiritual/intuitive revelations are often termed reductionism by even the most open and objective scientists and researchers, although their data points to the wondrous, numinous mystery of Life — a Mystery that ultimately cannot be fully known or quantized, but must be experienced; the World of the mystical and shamanic. We are simply quoting these examples to show that there is movement, convergence and even synergy on the planet between science and intuition. Mythos is created by worldviews, emotional investment, stances and "proven" paradigms. With the acceleration of information and the awakening of consciousness on the planet, things are changing rapidly. Be open and flexible. Evolution, by its very nature, is not always what you expect. The observer affects the observed. The map is not the territory.

Biophotons, in a more conventional linear model of reality, were discovered in 1923 by a Russian medical scientist named Professor Alexander G. Gurvich. He called them "mitogenetic rays."

In the 1930s, when a certain current and evolutionary goad was impacting the planet, the biophotonic process was being researched in Europe and the USA. A wave of covert alien contact had been experienced by certain factions at that point in the time-stream, and this of course is related to these "revelations." There have, in fact, been many holographic inserts into our reality during various points in the history of this planet by these "alien" influences, to shape human events and interactions. But now, humanity is awakening and all bets are off.

According to some sources, the concept of biophotons was "rediscovered" in the 1970s through experimentation and theoretical evidence by European scientists. We submit that this research had, in fact, continued "underground" since the 30's. The Russians were heavily into aspects of this research, and its relationship to scalar technology (knowledge is a two-edged sword).

In 1974 German biophysicist Fritz-Albert Popp validated the existence of biophotons, their origin within DNA and their coherence properties that were much like modern lasers. One does not have to stretch very far to also see the relationship to fiber optic technology as well. Popp explained what he saw as these biophotons' possible biological role in the biochemical processes, growth and differentiation within a living organism. Popp's biophoton paradigm has opened the door to many insights on the holistic nature of the life force interactions of living systems. A German organization, the International Institute of Biophysics, which is an expanding network of research laboratories in more than 10 countries, is coordinating and sponsoring frontier scientific research in this emerging field.

The DNA soundscapes can be used to connect these gates/portals/doorways by providing you with the sonic frequency maps which you can hold your focused intent upon during your meditation journeys, ultimately hopping on at some point to take a ride.

In our current paradigm, as alluded to above, we believe that there have been different currents and levels of research in many frontier scientific fields for many years, and many lifetimes. There are breakthroughs on all levels, and a cross-pollination of information has been occurring for many cycles of time. There has been a kind of "trickle down" effect from secret societies and research groups that have made substantial breakthroughs. The vast strata of such breakthroughs have been hidden from mankind. Only relatively small bits and pieces of information have been released, or allowed to rise to the surface of mankind's consciousness until the last few years. This in no way, shape or form negates the dedication and validity of the more external groups. Parallel development has been going on and there is much more than meets the eye. The light of illumination is shining brightly on the planet now, in many different approaches and in many different ways, for this is the time of the Gathering; the coming together of many teachings. What has been hidden, is being revealed. The biophoton paradigm is a key piece of the puzzle in beginning to see the relationship of the underlying scalar fields of this Harmonic Universe with the biophysical structures of 3D reality. When we look at the vast potential of the Unified Field from various angles — to the subatomic particle/waves, to the molecular, the receiver/transmitter/storage "antenna" of DNA and its accompanying messenger RNA, to the cells/cellular memory matrix that defines the organic systems

We have not as yet realized in a tangible manner, that we are connected to everything at once and communication within the superluminal transcends the so called limitations of the speed of light, space and time..

DNA Activation/Shapeshifter

within a living biophysical structure such as the human body temple, we can see they are endless.

We will elaborate for a moment on the DNA's antenna-like structure, for this is important. Viewed in one way, it is elongated in shape and thus can be considered a blade antenna, which is very efficient in receiving/sending electrical impulses. In another viewpoint, as seen from above, it can be said to have the form of a spiral ring and thus is a very good magnetic antenna. Electromagnetic energy is stored within the DNA molecule, bringing it into harmonic oscillation. It is designed this way. Perhaps now the concept of resonance begins to make even more sense. Light is electromagnetic energy composed of very small quanta, or packets, of energy and information. Biophotons transfer data not only throughout a particular organism, but through a network of light, the Language of Light, and convey this information through superluminal communication in what has been termed the morphogenetic field. We are also connected, in the empathic resonance of this communion, with the Telluric currents of GAIA (which can be thought of as mother earth's acupuncture meridians) and to all life. We are connected not only in this dimension but also through the chakric gateways/portals and through other spin points that relate to the acupuncture nodes and what has been termed the "assemblage point" within the luminous egg of the Castenada/Don Juan paradigm. These vortexes connect a vast matrix of interpenetrating Harmonic Universes in many dimensional states. Visualize the glittering web of these connections, feel the infinity of our unfolding in which we all are ONE. You can see from this perspective how the possibilities of remote viewing, teleportation and transmigration become possible.

According to some Russian research, the oscillation energy loss within the DNA resonator is incredibly small. The DNA is an organic superconductor, which can work at normal body temperature! The "mechanical" superconductors of scientific researchers must, at this point, be supercooled in the laboratory. Nature is so elegant. The ability for superconductors to store light was just recently discovered and has vast implications in memory storage of computing devices once the temperature challenge is solved. We in fact, believe that this obstacle has already been overcome by various Shadow projects that are already utilizing this technology in artificial intelligence and advanced weapons research. There's that two edged sword again, but we know the collective consciousness is turning the tide in the cycle of this New Atlantis and has made the choice for freedom, the affirmation of Life and of Love. Another interesting discovery that the Russian researchers found is that each DNA molecule, stretched end to end, is about two meters long and it has a natural frequency of 150 megahertz. A remarkable number, because this frequency is exactly in the range of our human radar, for telecommunications and microwave engineering. We use the same frequency range for communication and detection purposes. Hmmmmm

> *All languages emerged from transmissions/ communications from the DNA itself to further direct wo/mankind's evolution at certain points on the timestream...*

Another group of clever Russian scientists, in conjunction with linguists, studied the so-called junk/dormant DNA codex utilizing semantics (theory of the meaning of words) and syntax (rules for the setting up of words from letters), as well as the possible basis of its grammatical construction. Linguistics is the science of the structure of languages. It not only investigates the natural languages which developed in individual countries and cultures, but also artificial languages, which are used to program computers. What they found shook their former paradigms to the core. Through pattern recognition, they realized that the code follows the same structure underlying all human languages. Not the rules of a certain language (in this case the Russian one), but on a fundamental level in which all existing languages of mankind have comparable structures. A profound relationship was found between the structure of the genetic code and each existing language of mankind. For centuries researchers have sought the beginnings of the original human language — Pjotr Garjajev and his coworkers may very well have found it, within the DNA itself.

In one sense, it could be concluded that human languages are a reflection of the patterns within the DNA codex, specifically the 90-97% which as yet is overlooked by conventional science because they are not directly related to protein synthesis and other metabolic functions. That, in fact, all languages emerged from transmissions/communications from the DNA itself to further direct wo/mankind's evolution at certain points on the timestream. This is also why spoken word affirmations, uttered with feeling and intent, effect one's perceived reality. The DNA is a receiver and a transmitter. Remember the mythos of the Tower Of Babel, and the scattering of languages upon the planet? Within the morphogenetic field of the collective consciousness this relates to the frequency fences that were inserted by various alien influences who, among other agendas, did this to "dumb us down," and make us more malleable and controllable. Of course, that strategy is no longer working or necessary as the pathways of the web of light and strand overlays begin to re-connect and regenerate from the wavefront influence of a higher implicate order. You see, our base line potentials are being re-woven, re-connected, re-activated through stimulation from the galactic core. "They" (insert preferred belief system here) could not remove these baselines because there would be no lifeforce, we would have just been empty automatons, shells of flesh. The starseed roots of humanity's 12 strand metagalactic heritage run deep, far beyond this Harmonic Universe.

As Garajev and his team went deeper, they discovered that the vibrational matrix within the DNA followed the laws of nonlinear waveform-shaping, known since the mid 19th century as Soliton waves. Soliton waves are extraordinarily stable and may store information for a long time. Garajev concluded that the chromosomes work like solitronic, holographic computers utilizing biophotonic radiation. The Moscow researchers discovered that DNA substance in vivo (in the living fabric of an organism, not in the test tube) reacts to language-modulated laser light, even to radio waves, if one utilizes certain resonant frequencies. Now do you begin to see why we are using music/sound/frequency as a carrier wave? We will go further and say that the DNA codes are unlocked/activated through intent, and intent is, of course, energized by emotion and heartfelt feeling that "Modulate the Lifewave" of the scalar field potential.

Does this have deeper meaning to you now?

Scalar Field Dynamics =
field of information accessed by heartfelt feeling
that takes you ever deeper into Love.

The modulation of scalar field potential has many variations and is known by as many names as there are cultural worldviews and belief systems on the planet. It is known by the Yogis as Prana, the Chinese as Chi, the Polynesians/hunas as Mana, the Christians as Holy Spirit, the Russian's as Solitron Waves, William Reich's Orgone Energy, the Aether, Bioelectromagnetic Fields, and on and on.

A quote from an item in the Aug. 2, 2000 "What's New," electronic newsletter of the American Physical Society:

> *The director of the NIH Office of Alternative Medicine, Wayne Jones, is coauthor of a book called "Healing with Homeopathy." Most homeopathic remedies are so highly diluted that not a single molecule of the assumed active ingredient remains. So something beyond normal physics and chemistry must be invoked in order to explain homeopathic healing, assuming it is not simply the placebo effect.*
>
> *Jones says that healing is mediated by an elusive "biophoton," the quantum of the "bioelectromagnetic field," that triggers the familiar "butterfly effect" in chaos theory. "Quantum potentials" are "collapsed" by the thoughts of the healer, according to Jones, creating the healing biophotons.*

There may be hope for the NIH after all 🙂. We would suggest substituting the word "intent" for the word "thought" in the paragraph above. Quantum Potentials collapsed would be translated into, "the potentials of certain qualities are brought into manifestation through this intent, which directs energy through this frequency channel." We would also reiterate that this intent excites the scalar field potential, what we term Modulating the Lifewave, generating an electromagnetic connection between the healer and the receiver, directly proportional to the willingness and openness of said receiver. We would say that the biophotons are not created in the absolute literal sense, they manifest from the "Quantum potentials" — interactions of scalar fields, of rays or lines of directed "force." In addition, the energy that biophotons represent "flows back and forth" in communication and communion with other dimensional states of increasingly subtle matter and being.

Clara Bloomfield Moore has stated in her treatise Aerial Navigation (related to the Vanguard science of John Keely):

> *"Aether can be so divided as to generate lower and lower frequencies with resultant aggregations of energy, force and matter. Just as a prism converts white light (many combined frequencies) into what we perceive as single frequencies, so too can we use the phenomena of interference (collisions with other frequencies), to cause aether and other frequencies to be manipulated to produce energy, matter and various 'effects'."*

The concept of biophotons is an emerging paradigm of enlightened frontier science. Biophotons, or ultraweak photon emissions of biological systems, are electromagnetic particle/waves in the optical range of the spectrum — perceived as Light. In this sense, we are all light beings. All living cells of plants, animals and human beings emit biophotons which cannot be seen in normal 3D reality. This light emission is an expression of the energetic state of well-being and evolutionary unfoldment. German researchers have developed special equipment to measure these emissions, which is of special interest to us as the visual representation patterns of these generated displays of light dispersion may reveal much about the process of DNA Activation. Much of the current, openly available research is being done on this in Japan, Russia and Sweden. We imagine, although not much has literally come to light, that the Secret Government of this country is also engaged in similar explorations, as much relates to the information obtained from back engineered alien technology and biological material obtained. Again, this alien material was allowed to fall into certain hands, either as a ruse or an evolutionary goad — you decide!

In one current paradigm, biophoton light is stored in the living cells of the organism within the DNA molecules of their nuclei. We will go farther still, and say that biophotons also flow through the portals of the DNA from the other Harmonic Universes. A web of light received and transmitted by the DNA connects cells, tissues and organs within the body temple in a communication network matrix that literally sustains the life force of same. The dynamics of growth, renewal, evolution and structural differentiation are all functions and potentials of the organization of biophotonic field interactions. Consciousness, memory and perception are holographic qualities and states deriving from these fields of awareness and intent. We postulate that these organizing matrixes of biophotonic light, called The Language of Light, is the self organizing communication network that connects the levels of manifest reality through the various states and dimensions. This extends from the levels of flesh, nerve, gland and bone, to the spinning chakras, to the merkabic and sacred geometry of being, to the atomic, subatomic and superluminal — what have been termed the scalar fields.

For those of you willing to entertain the concept that the writers/creators of sci-fi and fantasy adventures often receive and translate channeled information, there is a very interesting correlation to all of this in the Stargate SG-1 Showtime series (1997-2007 TV Series). In this series, the Stargate is a teleportation device which links together a vast network of planets. Only portions of this information have been brought forth to the writers of this 'fictional' work. The cosmic travelers, in this series, move through the gate via wormholes. If one were to take the analogy further, one could relate our spiral DNA to the Stargate structure, and then take the intuitive leap that the DNA vortexes are also portals for connection, communion and travel through various dimensions of the Harmonic Universes. Also, that the holographic biophotonic network connects these vortexes of the body temple and their harmonic frequency reflections, the chakras and meridians, through a sacred geometry of connecting points. So rather than one gate, we have a vast series of interconnecting nodes within us, which increases the possibilities exponentially. The DNA soundscapes can be used to connect these gates/portals/doorways by providing you with the sonic frequency maps which you can hold your focused intent upon during your meditation journeys, ultimately hopping on at some point to take a ride. As the technique of Becoming the Music advances for you, you will be shown how to do this by your guidance in the steps and stages that you can handle.

From the East Indian Avatamsaka Sutra:
> *Far away in the heavenly abode of the great god Indra, there is a wonderful net that has been hung by some cunning artificer in such a manner that it stretches out infinitely in all directions. In accordance with the extravagant tastes of deities, the artificer has hung a single glittering jewel in each node of the net, and since the net itself is infinite in all dimensions, the jewels are infinite in number. There hang the jewels, glittering like stars of the first magnitude, a wonderful sight to behold. If we now arbitrarily select one of these jewels for inspection and look closely at it, we will discover that in its polished surface there are reflected all the other jewels in the net, infinite in number. Not only that, but each of the jewels reflected in this one jewel is also reflecting all the other jewels, so that the process of reflection is infinite.*

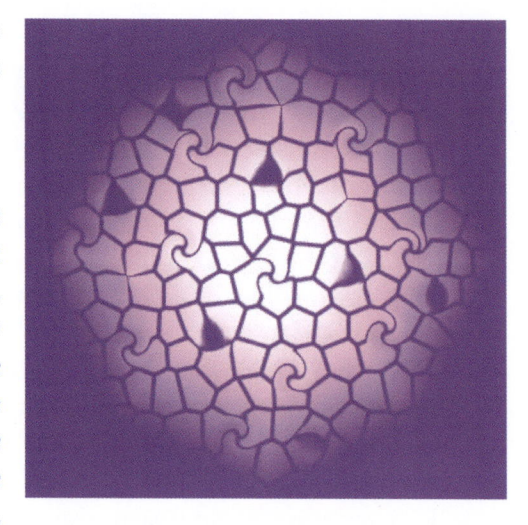

The Stargate technology in the Showtime series was introduced to Earth by the Goa'uld whose leader calls himself RA. RA, of course, being a solar deity, the Egyptian god of the Sun. Sun=Light. It is a large torus constructed of naquada. Naquada in the Stargate SG-1 mythos is a non-terrestrial mineral similar to quartz in general structure and is highly conductive. Remember the Russian research that we were speaking of earlier said that the DNA is a superconductor? Crystalline structures are excellent conductors/conduits for electric/electromagnetic/biophotonic flows.

From the American Journal of Complementary Medicine/Jim Oschman we read -

> *"It is already widely recognized that all the major constituents of living organisms may be liquid crystalline (Collings, 1990) - lipids of cellular membranes, DNA, possibly all proteins, especially cytoskeletal proteins, muscle proteins, and proteins in the connective tissues such as collagens and proteoglycans (Bouligand, 1972; Giraud-Guille, 1992; Knight and Feng, 1993). Recent nuclear magnetic resonance (nmr) studies of muscles in living human subjects provide evidence of their "liquid-crystalline-like" structure (Kreis and Boesch, 1994). However, very few workers have yet come to grips with the idea that organisms may be essentially liquid crystalline."* They conclude - *"We have proposed that the acupuncture (meridian) system and the DC body field detected by Western scientists both inhere in the continuum of liquid crystalline collagen fibres and the associated layers of bound water that make up the bulk of the connective tissues of the body. Acupuncture meridians may be associated with the bound water layers along oriented collagen fibres,*

which provide proton conduction pathways for rapid intercommunication throughout the body; while acupuncture points may correspond to gaps in the fibres or fibres oriented at right angles to the surface of the skin. The sum total of the electrical and electromechanical activities of the liquid crystalline continuum constitutes a "body consciousness" that works in tandem with the "brain consciousness" of the nervous system."

To finish our Stargate analogy, the Gate has a free-spinning inner ring incised with 39 glyphs — 3+9=12. The 12 strands of DNA. When one dialed in certain glyph sequences (restranding the codes, the strands being, in one sense, biophoton arrays) one could travel to and communicate with other worlds (or other dimensions) ;-).

The chi flowing in our bodies' energy channels/meridians is related to the node lines of the organism's biophoton field. The "prana" of Indian Yoga also arises from these electromagnetic biophotonic fields. The Kundalini energy, and its snakelike movement thru the spinal channels rises in an awakening being, is another process that we believe is connected to the "firing off" of biophotonic energy. As this flow makes a connection through the DNA with a stream of superluminal intra-dimensional energy from the wormhole chakra gateways to other Harmonic Dimensions, resonances are established. Yes, your chakras are doorways into multiple worlds and dimensions, along with their functions as placeholder spiral vortexes of certain energies and states of being in this reality.

DNA vortexes are also portals for connection, communion and travel through various dimensions of the Harmonic Universes.

Consider this — Plants nourish themselves from light. The leaf pigment chlorophyll is utilized in order to produce sugar from carbon dioxide and water using light. They take up energy and create an ordered structure from light particles (photons), which they integrate into their biophysical structure. Do you see why it can be important for the human body temple to receive nourishment directly from plant based material, and in particular such sources as greens, spirulina, chlorella, etc. It makes sense to utilize more raw and algae based foods in one's diet to begin to evolve the energetic structure of one's being, rather than to extract nourishment from so much dead dense flesh and processed foods, another step removed from the Source. One certainly may choose to transcend and transmute this lower vibrational quality or to rationalize that they do not care about this, that these restrictions impinge upon their freedom and their joy. However, one may find that the cost to the physical is not worth it while one, through the tantra of living, achieves such abstract skills of mastery as your Light Quotient increases. Center yourself and listen to what your body, not your emotions, is telling you — through feeling tones, through sensations, from your very DNA. If one still chooses to eat flesh foods, one should do their best to transform the vibrational quality and not be attached to what it represents. Denial often engenders repression and guilt, rather than growth. One only truly gives something up and lets go to make way for the new, when one has chewed through any remaining shreds of flavor, meaning and attachment. This applies to food, to habits, to lifestyles, to worldviews and to dead end relationships as well. Also, one can eat the most organic, most light-filled, vibrationally rich foods on the planet and still be unhealthy, diseased and out of balance. (more detailed info on this topic in our book The Secret to Abundance: ReJuva- see back of guide for more info) Because it's not just food, it's attitude. Being down on the world and on your life compresses and contracts your energetic biophotonic field. Now when we say, Light Quotient, or vibrational state, can you begin to see the connection? You can override the highest vibrational spaces, or the most loving healer, or the beauty of nature that could cause your very soul to sing, through your freewill. One becomes locked in a pattern of self importance, "My misery makes me special. I'm a suffering martyr that is so misunderstood. No one understands me because I am so unique and special, etc. etc." One becomes emotionally invested in depression, believing that is one's identity in a kind of self-referential feedback loop. One's reality will certainly mirror this, further reinforcing one's beliefs. There are countless variations possible in the creative art of self sabotage. You are Light and you are Love. When you get that, when you choose to affirm your life and act, trust and live more and more in that space, you will shift, you will rejuvenate, you will Become.

Feel the love in the pranic energy that you inhale through your breath and the vibrations you absorb through the sounds, sights and colors all around you. The objects that we surround ourselves with, the people we engage with, the music that we listen to, the food we eat — all is important, yet it is not. It depends on what we hold onto and what we allow ourselves to resonate to. Ultimately it is what sticks to us that holds the most power. True progress comes when we sincerely choose to evolve, to unfold and to grow — and not before. Begin to see the divinity in all things. There are different paths, yet all lead to the One. Choose what truly feels right for you, remove self deflection and diversion. Embrace the paradox of divergent beliefs. Accept within any given moment of true awareness the limitations of the forms and stances that you adopt, then seek to transcend them. Do the best that you can, with sincere intent, making allowances for your ups and downs and your fluctuations. Do the same for others, as well. When you hold judgment on anothers choices and beliefs, you hold density for yourself as well. The more you reach out to IT, the more IT reaches back to you. Celebrate your life. Connect with your cellular memory, with your DNA and you will be shown the Way in the Light, your inherent biophotonic nature. Through the soul's calling, as we awaken, we naturally gravitate to that which is life affirming, whatever that term truly means to each one of us. Our attitude shifts and each of us knows, in our heart of hearts, when we are being sincere with ourselves and when we are ready to embrace change.

Each of us has felt those special moments, after a wonderful meal prepared with care, or after making love, or any peak experience when one feels connected to All That Is. There is that glow from within, that gleam in the eyes, that feeling that one's cells are literally dancing. Because they are, in the sparkling light of the biophotonic emissions. Love and bliss are optimal carriers of this energy, through the "waveguides" of the body temple, the nervous system and its reflection in the subtle body — the network of nadis (pranic channels). As we begin to seek out more expansive, more joyful experiences, our DNA oscillates in resonance, our biophotonic field increases in radiance, the energetic state of the matter of our bodies begins to shift to a higher coherence, a higher implicate order. As we learn, through experience and through intent, by doing and not just talking, we ground this energy within the physical. We become placeholders for this energy. Each shines, in their unique way, in the Light and others can see the tangible results — in our abundance, in our love and in the creative, artistic expression of our lives. That is one tangible way change will ripple out, in waves of bliss, across the world.

This has been a relatively brief overview of the fascinating subject of biophotons. We recommend those of you who enjoy the science of things to continue your research in this area.

Effects & Benefits of DNA Activation using our Multidimensional Music

By the time of this update (5/2012), there are many different approaches to activating one's higher DNA strands. These methods or techniques are being taught by many different types of teachers/healers and educators. We want to be clear that we are speaking here about working with our soundscapes as the primary approach. Other techniques or a combined approach may produce similar results, of which we cannot speak to.

While every person will have a different experience using these soundscapes, we have found that there is some common ground. For those who resonate with this approach, there is an immediate awareness that the sounds are new and unusual to the ear, yet vaguely familiar. Along with this awareness comes a sense of deep resonance and a feeling of "coming home." If you can understand that these sounds emanate from vibrational realms that are deeply connected to The Source of All That Is, then this awareness of going home will make more sense to you. This connection, via sound, will awaken within you the knowledge that you have already developed as well throughout your many lifetimes. Through this music, we have been able to tap into our many lives in which we have used sound as a way to connect to the higher realms. It has taken considerable dedication, discipline and commitment to transmit this energy, as you might imagine.

Another very common experience, is that each time that you listen you become aware of new sounds and passages in the music. You will find that even over long periods of time, this will continue to be so. The sounds we design are created multidimensionally so that they actually release new frequencies/sounds as you evolve and increase your Light Quotient. This is why it maintains its level of newness even when one listens on a regular basis.

We are unable to make any definitive claims on the physical effects that are produced by listening to the music. We are sure that you can intuit through your visualization and imaginative faculties what effects high level integration will have on your physical, mental and emotional well-being. Our work is much more than coming back to a baseline wholeness, it is about transformation. When used by an aware explorer of consciousness, profound results can be achieved, but ultimately it is up to each individual to discover this.

We have listed some effects and benefits that people have reported while listening to these soundscapes. They are not scientifically validated, just common observations from those who are working with these soundscapes.

Imagine driving down a road in 3D hundreds of times, something shifts your energy one day, a deja vu or synchronicity, you see an unusual structure or anomaly that you have never seen before that triggers something within you, within your DNA, a sense of deeper recognition and connection. It is not that it wasn't there, it is that you just never considered approaching reality from that aspect and that angle. When you are able to tune the dial, so to speak, of your inner receiver, you will discover that there are an infinite number of stations, some familiar, some seemingly alien, but all connected to and a part of the wonder that is you. This will stretch and expand your being as you begin to catch a glimpse of your true multi-dimensional nature. Then in time, when you are balanced and ready, you may be able to merge and shapeshift into any state you so choose in loving communion, in the realization that all separation is ultimately an illusion. As we become these more expansive states, we may take on and integrate the expanded possibilities and abilities of these states, thus a way of the Tao for the modern age.

We will leave it up to those who are using the DNA CDs to determine what benefits you have received in your life. There are common effects and some that are truly unique to each individual. The following are some of the effects frequently reported to us. We also feel this list contains the qualities one can develop if they sincerely work with the LevelOne Series.

- More relaxed
- Less stressed overall
- Sleep better through night
- Deeper sleep
- Requires less sleep
- Enhanced dream activity
- Lucid dreaming ability increases
- Deeper meditations
- Intuitive awareness expands
- New levels of creative expression
- Consciousness becomes more fluid and open
- Extended periods of deep meditation
- Wake up more refreshed and renewed
- Physical Rejuvenation processes initiated
- Experienced healing processes in physical body
- Stronger connection to various forms of divine intelligence
- Increased ESP/psychic abilities
- Increase manifestation abilities
- More synchronistic events
- Overall feel happier
- Feel lighter, more energetic
- Become more aware of vibrational fields

Increase in remote perceptions
More in flow with all of life
Moving through emotional blocks easier
Spontaneous Healings
Enhanced Remote Viewing practices
Children & pets respond by being more calm and relaxed
Enhanced connections with nature and elemental realms

Before you consider moving on to the DNA L2 Program, you should be able to check off many of these items above, at least in varying degrees of accomplishment. Moving towards mastery in any of these areas is what the DNA L2 Program is for. By the time you have worked with the LevelOne series for a while, you will have come to a place where you have a good idea where you are directing your life path, so that you can choose to focus on a few key areas to attain mastery. This may occur through the music or a combination of accumulated techniques and processes that you have worked with. The following list are some of the potentials and possibilities that we are working on for the DNA L2 soundscapes. These are some of the things that those in the L2 program have suggested as potentials — sort of a wish list at this point. We won't know until the program is several years old what the possibilities really are. This list will expand as the collective energy of this level of the work expands.

Enhancement of all DNA LevelOne benefits
More direct connections with manifestations at a quickened pace
Advanced ESP abilities - telepathy, levitation, teleportation, transmutation, remote viewing, astral & dimensional travels, time travel
Tangible and direct contact with the Other (higher realms, ETs, UltraTs)
Increase of financial abundance in alignment with need for project development in alignment with planetary shifts
Amplified energetic support provided by group synergy to assist in grounding planetary missions
Quick release & resolve of negative imprints, events and situations
Magnified understanding of higher teachings
Increase of creative abilities to receive and process downloads from higher realms
Attainment of spiritual wisdom via direct transmissions of Light
More direct communications via clairvoyant and clairaudient abilities

> Greater clarity in dreaming states providing tangible guidance for waking state
> Dissolving of the veils between dimensional states
> Communion and direct communications with the Elemental Kingdoms
> To experience light as food, preparing the way to breatharianism
> Activate axiatonal light lines that extend from our meridians to infinity
> Full awareness of the matrix and to travel anywhere within and without
> See and ground the full spectrum of light and color, sound, smell, touch, taste

Listening Suggestions

You are about to embark on a journey of discovery and adventure, one that contains the essence and intent of true transformation. This work is for serious spiritual travelers who are ready to step up in walking their path of Light, fully dedicated to the process. It is also for those who know it is time to integrate their spiritual awareness into their life in a more profound and purposeful way.

This work is expansive, yet it is also grounded in real world principles to help you bring the highest spiritual teachings forth into tangible actions and manifestations on the 3rd dimensional level of reality. Paying bills, shopping, cleaning house, doing dishes are all part of the grounding and embodying these spiritual principles. Finding a balance in your life is the key to this unfolding journey.

Depending on your comprehension of this subject, some of what we are about to share may not fit within your current frame of reference. Allow your consciousness to be open to new possibilities, step out of old boxes and step fully into the Light of your becoming. These soundscapes emanate from advanced teachings of using sound for the transformational process; that of shifting from 3rd dimensional human towards building a body of Light, embodying the consciousness of an Avatar in service, shifting into 5th dimensional reality and all ascension and conscious immortality dynamics. It is important to respect the process and not rush through your initial first pass with the 4 soundscapes. Allow your full being to integrate each one before moving on. Consider 7 listening sessions as a place to begin this adventure, but often it is much more than that to allow the frequencies to be assimilated on all levels of your bioenergetic matrix.

It always depends on where one is on their evolutionary journey before they begin listening. Only you can make that assessment by observing yourSELF from a higher perspective. If you can listen to the soundscape in a deep meditative state and journey through the dark and light passages while holding a higher state of awareness of the divinity within all states of duality, then move on to the next. But if you find that you are being challenged by areas in the music that push emotional or physical triggers deep in your being, then you need to spend time to recapitulate that energy further before moving on. If events in your life are suddenly shaken up, falling apart or dramas have increased, then you need to tend to that energy first before accelerating further. You may need to take breaks at times and back off or listen to something more benign, like our Healing or Sanctuary CDs (see back of guide). This is what they are for, to help you soften the process when you need to ease through your current transition. The Odyssey CD (see back of guide) can also be used to help you balance your chakras and expand your auric fields in preparation for multidimensional shamanic journeys. This CD can be used throughout your process to help you quickly move back into higher states of balance. If you work with the Odyssey CD for a few weeks before you really dive into the DNA Series, you will establish a good baseline balance state which you can return to as needed.

Once you have made it through all 4 soundscapes for your first pass, then you can listen in any order that you feel guided, as well as putting them on a multi changer and letting them cycle through. It is important that you have a strong connection with your higher self and guidance teams or whatever you may call your connection to the Infinite Source as you begin this journey. This connection will be needed during some of the more challenging passages. The AYD #1/Shamanic Journeys DVD Training Program (see back of guide) was created to help you develop a solid spiritual foundation. This will assist you in greatly deepening your experiences with this work. If you have not done much spiritual development, then this DVD is highly recommended as a place to start along with the soundscapes. As for "working" with the music, it is important that the music is played loud enough on a good external speaker system so that the body feels the music as well as hears it. MP3s are not recommended for the deeper work as they have many of the higher and lower frequencies removed due to the compression format. If you convert the CDs to be played on your Ipod type players, we suggest you use the .wav or .aif formats so as not to lose any frequencies. Be sure to work with the Become the Music technique available on our website as a flash movie or on our AYD #2 DVD Training Program. This is the primary technique you want to begin with as you start your adventures with the soundscapes. The deeper you can let go into full immersion of becoming sound, the more profound your results and experiences will become. This DVD will also expand your work greatly in learning how to work with this sound for your transformational work. By working with both of these DVD's along with the music, you will be developing some advanced skills in shamanic journeying work. Additional studies on shamanic techniques is also advised.

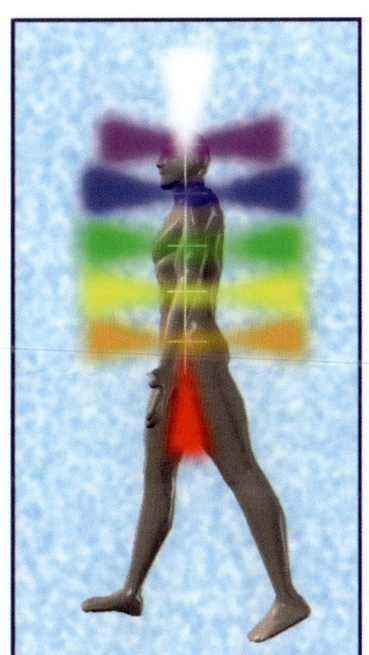

Just start this adventure by listening to the sounds, meditate, listen some more and all will begin to resonate on the deeper levels of your being. You will soon be guided to listen in certain ways or times that fit within your life patterns. Listening quietly in the background gradually builds up supportive level frequencies in your environments where you live, play and work. As the music permeates the cellular levels of your living spaces, it allows for greater levels of harmony with all aspects of your life. Whoever and whatever inhabits that space begins to lift vibrationally. Relationships between humans and animals and plants will all begin to take on new depths of Love and connection.

Listening during sleep time is a very powerful way to work with this music. You can play them throughout the night at a low volume to assist in your nocturnal adventures. Upon going to sleep and awakening, it is good to spend time just engaged in the sounds for deeper processing of dream sequences, assisting energetic manifestations/visualizations and deepening meditative states.

We highly recommend that you reread the Companion Guide from time to time to evolve your intellectual understanding of the process and your overall relationship to this material. There are feeling tones within these word pictures that will begin to emerge. Patterns once hazy will reach a new state of clarity when you come back and read the information again and yet again.

For those who already understand the majority of this, welcome home! Understand that this is not meant to create a separation between those who already comprehend this work and those who are just beginning. We are all at different levels of understanding about the whole and this is one piece of the puzzle that we offer from our evolving perspective.

We are proposing that you consider a new way of viewing your reality as a multidimensional consciousness within matter and redirect your intent so that DNA Activation subtly becomes a main theme of your spiritual growth work. This orientation will bring all aspects of your explorations into a seamless tapestry that becomes the full potential of what you are. When you initiate conscious communication with your DNA, the core level organizational matrix of your being, multiple dimensions of depth and meaning will unfold in everything that you experience.

The following are creative suggestions that are offered from the transmissions we have received and explored in our communications with our DNA matrix and through that matrix, the connection to our Higher Selves, our group soul monad and beyond. You will gain much from following them, however feel free to adapt and improvise upon these exercises in alignment with what you believe is possible within your given situation. With this LevelOne Series of DNA Activation music, we give you the seed of a new beginning that will open you to new possibilities. It is an initiation of great importance and magnitude, so treat it and the process with reverence and respect. The clarity with which you step into this journey, will be reflected back at you in many ways. Be aware that you can no longer obfuscate the truth of who you are or what you have been throughout all your incarnations. When you step into the pure frequencies of Light and Love within these soundscapes, these hidden places will be revealed. The mirror will be reflected back at you and you will need to be able to deal with many aspects of yourself that have been eluding you for some time. If you were not ready for this step on your evolutionary path, then your guidance would not have brought you to this teaching. Always remember that we are here to assist you in various ways as you walk this path — you are not alone. We offer free teleconferences, online chats and deeper spiritual guidance sessions at The 3rd Eye website (see back of guide for more info).

1 THE FIRST TIME: Before you do your first initial listening adventure while in a deep meditative state, we recommend that you prepare with focused intent, yet with a sense of relaxed anticipation. You will achieve more empathic resonance to the music by achieving a state of calmness and peace before beginning the process. Set aside several hours, create a sacred space and be sure that you will remain undisturbed during this entire experience. Consider bathing to cleanse the auric field and do some gentle yoga stretching to begin relaxing the body. It is important to make your listening space as positive and uplifting as possible. You may feel the need to smudge, to utilize aromatherapy or other personal sacred rituals to cleanse your environment. Invoke a feeling of love, safety, sanctuary and protection with deep feeling and sincerity. Connect to whatever aspect of All That Is that you relate to, with whatever methods feel right for you. The more you put into the process, the more will be returned to you.

Use the highest quality CD player that you have. We do not recommend headphones for this first session, as you want the sounds to reflect from the acoustic space of the entire room, surrounding you in a powerful vibrational matrix. This is not to say that you should never explore with headphones, as the movement of the soundfields within your headspace adds a different dimension to the experience. Just not for the first time, as it is important that your entire energy space be immersed in the frequencies. In addition to hearing the music, it is very important to FEEL as deeply as you are able; let your physical body, down to the cellular level, blend with the sounds and joyfully dance to the resonant frequencies. Let go, allowing your consciousness to travel on these waves of sound and energy patterns — truly step into Becoming the Music (see flash movie on website homepage or the AYD #2 DVD Training Program). Let yourself be guided by your own inner knowingness, while also being mindful of where you are travelling. Use your shamanic skills if you have them. If you do specific meditations, breathing exercises or chakra balancing work, do these first to prepare yourself for the journey. The Odyssey CD is excellent for balancing the chakra system and expanding your awareness of the entire auric field, so you can play that first if you have it. We also have an MP3 guided journey on our website to help you balance your chakras if you don't have the AYD #1 DVD.

The DNA CD package design was created from the same source as the music. We suggest that you spend some time viewing this as strong intent is also reflected in this piece of art. The colors, shapes and patterns all contain deeper messages for your unfolding path. Imagine the cover art as a holographic image, an energy field, a matrix of sound & harmonics surrounding you as you stand in the center. (see visual animation of this in our AYD #1/Shamanic Journeys DVD Training Program) The energetic flow of the poems on the back of each CD reflect the music inside. As you listen, ask your guidance to reveal the deeper teachings within the poetic flow.

If you have not had any specific DNA Activation work done prior to starting your work with these soundscapes, then we recommend you work with our guided journey to Activate the DNA. This is also available on our AYD #1/Shamanic Journeys DVD Training Program as well as an MP3 download. Before doing this, you should deeply consider the commitment you are making to your self. Additional studies on this topic are recommended to enhance your knowledge. See our recommended book list at VisionaryMusic.com/dna-books.html

2 SHAMANIC JOURNEYING: Whatever form of shamanic journeying you choose to do, you can use the DNA CDs as part of your explorations. These soundscapes are created to provide a safe, supportive energy grid and sanctuary around your space while you explore other dimensions from an altered state of consciousness. You can travel to lower, middle and upper worlds easily using the soundscapes as a bridge to any destination you set your intentions towards. This is one of the most powerful techniques you can use while working with this music. Study additional information on this subject to enhance your experiences and to build up your knowledge.

3 GUIDED JOURNEYS/MEDITATIONS: We offer guided journeys to begin your explorations and to enhance your experience with these CDs. They are offered on our AYD DVD Training Program as well as MP3 downloads on our website. You may, of course, also work with guided journeys recorded by others, as these soundscapes will enhance any of those experiences. Guided journeys are a great way to focus your energy while letting someone gently guide you through the process.

4 PLAYING IN YOUR ENVIRONMENTS: In addition to listening with conscious awareness throughout the journey, you may also choose to let the music play in the background of the environments where you live, work, play and drive. As you become more aware of the subtleties in the matrix of the Universal Energy Field, you will be able to sense how the sounds create vibrational patterns in your living spaces. As you are enhancing and unfolding the potential of your personal energy field and activating the dormant codes in your DNA, you begin to increase your manifestation abilities by building a more cohesive base of empowerment within your auric field. In essence, you are increasing your Light Quotient. By extending this to the environments that you spend your time in, you start expanding your sphere of influence in all that you seek to manifest. Harmony will manifest in your interactions with others and the world around you. By surrounding yourself as often as possible with these frequencies, the Universal Laws of Attraction are magnified and magnetized. A note of caution to those who may not be able to maintain the appropriate level of awareness while driving or working — work towards using the CDs in these environments gradually and gracefully.

5 **LISTEN WHILE YOU SLEEP/LUCID DREAMING:** These CDs have a profound and positive effect when played throughout the night while you are sleeping. It is best to have a multi changer CD, so you can put all of the CDs in the player and put on continuous play. When utilized in this way, you will achieve a much deeper and more restful state of sleep, refreshing and rejuvenating the physical vehicle to the cellular level and beyond. If you relax into the process, any insomnia problems may very well dissolve in a cloud of pleasant dreams. Use them to shamanically explore your day and meditate with prior to falling asleep and the same upon awakening. As you wake up, allow yourself some extra time to process the night's astral travels and dreamscapes and to seek higher guidance on your journeys. If you are working with lucid dreaming, the energetic space that these CDs create will certainly take that process to a new level. You may program yourself before going to sleep to work on your DNA and/or any other areas of your life that you would like to seek guidance on. During the night, if you awaken, you will be able to touch into the soundscape and be guided into many wonderful insights about your life path by consciously following the sounds back into the landscape of your dreams. The music will assist you in maintaining connections to the higher dimensions and make it more difficult for the lower astral worlds to penetrate your field. Progressive dream adventures will mirror back to you the spiritual work you are doing. They will evolve each time as you take back more awareness of your personal power. Keep a journal at your bedside to record your experiences, as these interesting patterns will eventually emerge that will lead you to deeper understanding of your current incarnational focus.

6 **WORKING WITH OTHER DNA ACTIVATION TECHNIQUES:** Consider finding someone who is in your area, or coming to your area, that offers a workshop in DNA Activation to broaden the spectrum of your understanding on this subject. There are many different approaches available now and there are several teachers who are traveling around the planet offering these workshops. Doing this will enhance your experience while working with these CDs by consciously integrating different facets of this knowledge in your unfolding process. Remember all these different approaches will have gems of truth that resonate deeply with you and some will not. This is not a reflection on the teacher per se, just part of the many facets of Source that are being reflected at this time. The music becomes what you put into it, so use it to follow the truths that are important and specific to your path and purpose for incarnating at this time. Check our website or Google for teachers that offer DNA Activation workshops in your area or online. Choose the path that feels right for you. We also offer various types of spiritual guidance and vibrational healing sessions, as well as DNA Activations with the soundscapes at The 3rd Eye website (see back of guide for more info). The AYD #1 DVD includes an animation and guided journey on this process.

7 **RECOVERING PASTLIFE MEMORIES:** By setting your intention to discover pastlife memories, you can allow your consciousness to travel back through the time stream to locate this information. The soundscapes will support this process in many amazing ways. Stay focused and relaxed, keep a pen and paper or recorder handy so you can take notes as you travel. The music can act like a bridge to connect you to your higher guidance, if you will allow it to do so. Playfully shift in and out of mental awareness during your travels, so that your guidance can take you into the vibrational realms of information. Travel with the feeling tones as you are guided, let the music stimulate the information, visions, feelings and sensations to come forth. Follow the energy flow with your physical and mental awareness. All of the information of your incarnations, both past and future, of parallel lives, selves and other extensions of your group soul is available to you within your DNA and its communion with your cellular memory — your Akashic Records. Keep your intentions clear and within the essence of your resolve the insights will surface. The mists of forgetting will clear, in the time frame that is in alignment with your growth and your soul's highest aspirations. If you are working with a therapist to help you in your regression work, consider taking this CD along to enhance the process. If you are a therapist, you can use this music to deepen the process for your clients. We also offer core level pastlife readings that can release some of the initial visions to get you started on unfolding these energetic imprints. Refer to The 3rd Eye in the back of the guide.

8 **MANIFESTATION:** Start by being very clear on what the essence is of that which you are wanting to manifest in alignment with the highest good of all concerned. This means rather than focusing on the small details of something, you bring all the small pieces together into an overall umbrella of all aspects of what you desire. Capture the feeling tones of what it would be like to have that manifestation. Then as you start listening to the soundscape, let it evoke ideas, visions and courses of action that will assist you in the accomplishment of this goal. It is like harmonically matching up the pieces of the puzzle, so that they all fit together perfectly. If you are honest with yourself and remain open to new possibilities, insights may very well emerge that will both surprise and delight you. You can write these down to monitor your unfolding process. Also, ask your guidance to show you the blocks and potential challenges that you may face as you move towards your goal. Ask to be shown your core level belief systems that will either enhance or prevent this manifestation. Along the way, ask to be shown the steps necessary in the 3D world that you need to do in order to accomplish this goal. Act upon them with sincerity and commitment, synchronicities will occur, doors will open and the path will be made clear. Now is the time to act, for the energy of the planet is accelerating. Trust and faith are the bridge that you must travel to a new reality. You know what truly brings you joy. Following your true bliss will add to the Light of Planetary Evolution, as you are initiated into the path of balanced co-creation with Source. Let the music help you unfold these teachings. The Universe Loves you unconditionally. Feel this boundless Love and Light as it moves in pulsing waves through every fiber of your being. All the illusions, anger, resentment, all feelings of hurt and limitation now dissolve in the glow of this sparkling light. Be grateful for the opportunities that you have been given for growth. Be grateful for the wonder of your life, your awareness, your Love and connection to Source. Do this often, with impeccable intent and miracles will surely manifest in your life. Refer to our book called The Secret to Abundance: ReJuva for more info on manifesting in all areas of your life (see back of guide).

9 **HEALING THE PHYSICAL BODY:** For these sessions, you will want to start off by surrounding yourself with White Light, calling forth any special forms of guidance that you work with, ask for the presence of healers or master teachers from the higher levels to assist your in your process. Use whatever techniques, ceremonies or rituals you are most comfortable with. Focus your awareness on the specific part of the body that you are doing the healing work on and increase the Light Quotient in that area of your body. There is a piece on this in the AYD #1 DVD to help you work on this. Channel Light energy, using your breath, in (inhale) from your crown chakra to your heart center and out (exhale) your arms to your hands, placing your hands upon the area where you wish to send healing. With your conscious intent, send the music soundscapes into this area and let the energy travel around as needed. Follow this energetic thread with your consciousness and go as deeply into a state of relaxed meditation as you can. Use the breath in the area of healing to relax the muscles or tissues, letting go of any tension. Connect this area to higher realms and sense the higher blueprint of health and vitality envelop it. It is OK if you eventually fall asleep as your higher guidance will take over the process for you. Ask for assistance in understanding the deeper truths available to you within this healing process. Without judgment of self, take responsibility for the creation of the imbalance, make peace with yourself and any others that you are holding negative emotions towards and let go into Love, for Love heals all. At times the DNA music can be too intense for doing healing work on the physical body if it is experiencing pain or discomfort. During these times, we recommend using the Healing or Sanctuary CD (see back of guide).

10 **MUSICAL EXPLORATION:** You do not always have to DO something specific with these soundscapes, you can just enjoy them for their unique and creative multidimensional content. Try listening on different sound systems as well; in particular, use headphones on occasion and if you have the opportunity to experience a sound table/chair, you will truly enjoy their fullest potential as they were created in this type of environment — see The Odyssey Sound & Light Temple on our website – VisionaryMusic.com/odyssey/odyssey.html. Let your mind and etheric body wander around within the soundscapes and just LET GO. You will be pleasantly surprised and uniquely entertained!

11 **SPACE TRAVEL:** One intention when using these soundscapes is to travel inside the body to activate and resonate with the DNA codex and its connection to the sub-atomic, other dimensions of matter and beyond. You will also find that you can travel out into space and explore its depths within the third eye of your higher imagination. Remember what we have said previously — the DNA is a receiver and a transmitter. Take a ride on a visionary spaceship. Visualize the spin of your Merkabah. Voyage out into the multiverse and the infinite adventures that await. Connect with fellow space travelers.

12 **ASTRAL TRAVELS, OBE, TELEPORTATION, LEVITATION, TELEPATHY:** Many people who seek out this type of exploration are looking for a deeper way to connect to The Source, finding that if they can release their connection to physical matter for a period of time that they will discover some powerful truths about the very nature of reality and their existence. It is also a form of metaphysical entertainment and amusement. If you use the music as a guide and a bridge to and from these spaces, you can learn how to control the experience and create the sensations that you seek. We recommend that you research these techniques before you set your intention to engage. The music provides you with the frequency maps throughout the harmonic Universes, so as you learn to hold higher states of focused attention during these adventures, the more ability you can develop over time. It requires patience and practice ultimately. These abilities will be a natural part of our being as we continue to evolve into the 5th World. Each successive series of DNA soundscapes will increase your abilities in these areas exponentially.

13 DEVELOPING PSYCHIC ABILITIES: Use the music to guide you towards expanding your field of awareness, stepping out beyond the 3rd dimensional realms of limited reality. Opening the sixth senses to perceive more expanded realities takes diligence, patience and practice. Start this journey with learning how to balance the charkas, as without a balanced chakra system, distortions can occur in your energy field that will leave you feeling off balance and unable to handle the energetic flows you will experience when you expand beyond normal 3D frequencies. Then you can begin expanding the auric field layer by layer, extending your awareness first to the room that you are in and then to the house, building/home, neighborhood, city, state, country, planet, atmosphere, solar system, galaxy, the Universe. By doing this exercise, you will increase your range of awareness and sensitivity to all that is going on around you, which is what opens up the psychic centers. This in and of itself, will start to awaken your 6th sense abilities. Use the music soundscapes as building blocks to assist you in this process. If you are doing psychic/intuitive readings at this time, use these soundscapes as background music to help you and your clients maintain connection to the higher realms. Additional reading and studying on this subject is recommended to achieve the best results. If you are just beginning, remember that it takes time for these gifts to unfold. However, if you have had significant pastlife training in these areas, it could open up very quickly. Set the pace with your higher guidance team so that you can integrate these openings with your current world. The AYD #2 DVD will help you greatly in developing this work.

14 FIRST AWAKENINGS TO THE LIGHT: If you are relatively new to tuning into The Light for your spiritual understanding and awareness, you can use these CDs to initiate you into your first awakening experience. Make the event special, create a sacred space, connect with your guidance and ask that if it is time for you to awaken a new level of your being to make it so. Lie down and breathe deeply, inhaling the sounds into your entire being. Feel into the vibrational tones within the music and let go deeper and deeper. Feel the physical body relaxing and start sensing all the energy that surrounds you. Ask your Higher Self to infuse you with a new level of Light and let it be so. Breathe it in. We really recommend that you work with the AYD #1 DVD Training Program to help you build a strong spiritual foundation for this work.

15 CONNECTING WITH YOUR HIGHER SELF: If you have not already connected with your Higher Self or if you feel your connection could be enhanced, we recommend that you use this music to create the space to make this very important and powerful connection. Your Higher Self is that aspect of you that is all wise and knowing. It resides on the higher dimensional levels of reality, so it always has the higher perspective on what is going on in your life. By consciously connecting and engaging with this inner voice, you are able to navigate through many of lifes situations with greater peace and inner knowing that all is in divine order. We cannot stress enough that this relationship is crucial to the success you will attain with this work. Establishing this relationship will assist you in your multidimensional travels by providing you with constant awareness of the greater scope of what is occurring. We offer you a meditation that you can work with to guide you towards deepening this connection. It is available on the AYD #1/Shamanic Journeys DVD Training Program and as an MP3 soundfile on our website. The Healing CD is also very good for this process.

16 **ASCENSION/DESCENSION PROCESSES:** Let these soundscapes take you in either direction based on your desire to explore both realities fully. The music provides a mapping to these dimensional states. Set your intention clearly in your mind and let the music gently guide you up or down the spiraling DNA ladder to ascend beyond 3D reality or to descend deeply into the world of matter. It is amazing the similarities you will find as you travel in either direction, like a mobius strip of information and meaning that connects the dimensional octaves. You can use a simple counting system to direct the focus of your experience into these realms. Further study on this is suggested.

17 **REMOTE VIEWING, TIME TRAVEL:** Set your target in your mind of where you want to go prior to putting the CD on. Once you are clear about where you want to go and what you want to discover when you get there, put the music on. You might want to dowse or muscle test to determine which CD would be most appropriate for your traveling. Either record what you see or write it down. Let yourself freely associate what comes to you without judging it. In time, you will be able to perfect this process. Additional studies are required to master this technique.

18 **HEALING SESSIONS WITH OTHERS:** Massage/Bodywork/Regression/Psychotherapy, etc.: Assisting another person in their healing process is a wonderful experience as long as your intentions are clear and pure of heart. Always remember that you can support them with additional Light and assist them by creating a space of unconditional Love, but it is up to them ultimately to choose to accept the energy offered. Playing these CDs during any type of healing session will deepen the experience and allow them to travel off with the soundscapes into the quantum levels of reality where the deepest healing takes place. Let them drift off and go to sleep if necessary. Most often, they will drift in and out of consciousness during the session. The music will assist the healer as well to stay focused and deeply connected to the Higher Source of healing energy. Whatever type of healing service you offer, these CDs will deepen and enhance the connection your clients receive from their session. Let the music play in the background or use it to guide your client into various spaces for further explorations. Be sure to bring your CDs with you to any healing session work that you are doing, as they will enhance your experience. For professional healers, we do ask that if you use our soundscapes as a primary focus with your work that you consider tithing back to us on occasion in gratitude for their added gift to your work.

19 DEVELOPING CLAIRVOYANT ABILITIES: These CDs will activate the pineal/pituitary area of the chakra system, which will in turn stimulate visual imagery. By directing the sounds and frequencies into this area of your body, you can enhance the process by stating your intentions to awaken more of your clairvoyant abilities. Look into the dark spaces and call for colors and images as the music gently guides you into different landscapes. Learn how to develop the ability to see without looking! When an image starts to form, if you try to hard to see it, you will lose it — learn a state of relaxed observation. Use your imagination to assist the process and create new images based on your thought patterns — explore. This music will stimulate visual imagery to occur, you need to be the one to interpret what comes forth from your consciousness.

20 BREATHWORK/REBIRTHING: If you are doing any specific kind of deep breathing exercises, we recommend that you definitely combine these techniques with the DNA CDs. Breathing deeply into the sounds, tones and modulations will really help to release some of the DNA information/cellular memories within. Conscious breathing, the inflow and outflow of Prana, increases the effectiveness of the CDs tenfold. For teachers focused on breathwork, you can add these soundscapes to your collection to guide the group deeper into the process. We do ask that if you use our soundscapes as a primary focus with your work that you consider tithing back to us on occasion in gratitude for their added gift to your work.

21 READING/STUDYING: When you sit down to read, take a few moments to check in to your DNA level and set the intention that what you are about to read is going to be assimilated by your consciousness. If it is technical info, ask to remember easily and to absorb the details on higher levels so that you can speed read and still absorb the important data. If you are reading spiritual material, ask that what is for your Higher Good be received and to block out any material that is not important for your path at this time. Ask your guidance to teach you discernment about the material being presented. As you read, take breaks and close your eyes, allowing the soundscapes to unfold the information to you vibrationally. You can take off into a deeper meditation also for an inner teaching and expansion of the subject matter received. Let the music be your guide.

22 ARTS/CRAFTS/PAINTING/SCULPTING/WRITING: Many artists already work with music as a background enhancement to their creative process. Consider consciously working with these soundscapes to bring forth a piece of art as you are guided. Let the sounds and melodies move your hands, paintbrush or digital stylus to create a masterpiece, a living expression of your unfoldment. If you are a writer, allow the words to flow with the pulsing of the music, breathe deeply, and let the information emerge from the deepest levels of your imagination. The potentials and possibilities are endless.

23 PLANT TEACHERS/PSYCHEDELICS: Whatever form of shamanic journeying you choose to do, you can use the DNA CDs as part of your explorations, including the usage of shamanic plant teachers. These soundscapes are created to provide a safe, supportive energy grid and sanctuary around your space while you explore other dimensions from an altered state of consciousness. When using altered substances, allow these soundscapes to provide a cohesive resonant frequency map to guide your journey into the Light even when visiting some of the lower worlds. The knowledge within these frequencies will be amplified, so we caution you to use mature judgment. We recommend these journeys be done with a reliable sitter present, if you choose to use them together. We do not recommend this for beginners or those not already experienced in this type of altered state exploration. DO NOT use if you are in an emotionally unbalanced state as it will be amplified tenfold with this music. With that said, one of the reasons we created the music was to replace the need to ingest any substance that alters the consciousness. Rather than take the burn on the physical body, we find it preferable to attain these states via the music alone. We find it to be a more balanced, more direct way of communing with the other realms and we are able to retain more of the information received, ultimately making it more tangibly useful in our 3D world.

24 **COMMUNING WITH NATURE:** Using these CDs while communing with nature can be a very powerful experience and Vision Quest. Take your player and go for a walk in the park or sit at the beach or watch the full moon. The music will also interact with the nature around you, so if you can play them out in an expanded forest environment where you are completely surrounded by nature's wonders, attune yourself to the music and then merge with the trees, birds and animals of the forest. Ask your guidance to show you the DNA patterns of nature. Listen to the sounds that the forest will reflect back to you. If you are into Shamanism or Native American teachings, be aware of messages from power animals and earth, air, wind, fire, water, sun, moon and the stars above resonating with your crystalline biology.

25 **TANTRIC LOVEMAKING:** Blending your energy with another in a loving act of sexual expression using tantric or similar techniques can be a very powerful experience that can lead to some of the highest states of bliss and joy. Add the intention to the process that as you venture in and through these blissful states of ecstasy while listening to the music, you allow the vibrations and sounds to release within your DNA the codes that will allow you to experience more of these sensations in your daily life. Awaken new pulsations in the physical body and anchor the sensations in your consciousness, letting the music assist you through the denser places of fear in relation to any of your repressed sexual feelings. Tantra in its highest sense, is one of the most empowering paths to the soma of physical immortality.

26 **CLEANSING/DETOXING PROCESSES:** Whatever form of cleansing or detoxing program that you are embarking upon, consider adding several listening sessions with the DNA music to assist in further clearing the body of toxins. Set up several different kinds of sessions during this period of time to deepen the effects of the program of cleansing and rejuvenation that you are working with. Travel into your DNA level and speak to it about the specific organ or system that you are focusing on at the time. Ask to initiate a deeper process of renewal and to remove any toxins that are preventing the organ/system from functioning at its optimal level of health. If you have the ability to take a hot bath, using clay, herbs, aromas to enhance the process, play the music in the background to assist in taking the process all the way to the DNA level. If you are doing colonics, detox baths, ozone steams, etc., take the CDs with you to assist in your release process.

27 LIFE RECAPITULATION: This is a very powerful and important technique that we recommend you do frequently throughout your life to reclaim lost energy. Traveling backwards in time, recovering experiences and situations in your life that hold emotionally depleting content and infusing them with higher Light to transform to a more Loving vibration is a potent technique for building the Light Quotient. Eventually you will want to travel all the way back to your birth and then even beyond that to significant pastlife imprints that still hold power and karmic threads of energy within your field. Use the music as a gentle guide taking you into the different scenarios you have experienced in your life, see them deeply for what they were then and are now. Then ask for higher guidance on the whys and hows of their manifestation. Listen for the deeper teachings to emerge and then infuse these situations with Light in order to transcend and move beyond them. The point of power is in the present. If you believe you can actually change the past by visualizing a different, more enlightened outcome, you will literally at some point be able to alter that dynamic, thereby changing the flow of your present and your future. This takes impeccable practice, but is entirely possible with directed intent. Use the Recapitulation Journal in the back of this guide to trigger memories and stimulate thoughts. Create a special ceremony for capturing and then releasing the energy using your breath. The music will become invaluable in this process and considered one of the most potent tools for assisting in the release of density and the transformation into Light.

28 PHYSICAL EXERCISE: Whatever program of exercise you are doing, you can use these DNA CDs to add a new wave of energy and vitality into the process. They may not be appropriate for some aerobic programs, but certainly for yoga, pilates, tai chi, qigong, rites of rejuvenation, falun dafa, tensigrity and other movement work. You can take any of these to a new level by incorporating the awareness of going to the DNA level of your being and infusing yourself with more Light and personal empowerment to increase the overall effects of the exercises that you are doing.

29 CHARGING WATER: To enhance the vibrational quality of the water that you are drinking or any flower/gem/vibrational essences that you may be taking, place a glass or bottles on or in front of your speakers. Play each CD in succession to charge the water or if you are working with a specific CD, charge it for at least 4 hours. Begin this process by stating your intention, calling on your guides to assist in this process. This will cluster the water in a higher geometric matrix and infuse it with living energy. As you drink the water or take the drops, again affirm your intent to activate the DNA using the water as a catalyst to deliver radiant well-being to the cellular matrix of your crystalline body. Remember that we are 85-90% water, so taking in this vibrational essence in to the body will amplify and enhance the resonance of the music.

About the Creators . . .

The following bios are expanded upon in the FREE PDF Info Packet that we offer on our website. There is also additional information on the name Shapeshifter and how we received it. If you have not already requested this, please email us at evolve@visionarymusic.com.

Gary Chambers/ShapeshifterOne:
A Musician's Quest

At the age of 5, sitting at the piano, Gary explored his emerging fascination with the sciences — astronomy and microbiology — by closing his eyes and immersing himself in the visual landscapes of his imagination. Young ShapeshifterOne spent countless hours either peering through the microscope at the wonders within a drop of pond water, or gazing at the stars and imagining what life on other worlds might be like. At a very early age, he learned of the Kingdom within. A connection was sensed, was felt, to a vast cosmology encompassing all things. Glimpses of other lives appeared in his consciousness, ephemeral memories of other times. There were contacts throughout his early childhood, with mysterious others, both in the waking world and in dreams. Teachings were given, information was absorbed. His interest in science turned to an interest in science fiction/fantasy, metaphysics, quantum physics and spiritual philosophy and he would spend large portions of his free time reading and absorbing thousands of books. His flights of imagination often contained valid information that would later become a part of the teachings he would offer to humanity to assist in this current phase of our collective evolution through sound and a higher understanding of the transformational aspects of frequency based music. He does not read or write music, he becomes the sound. He is immersed in sonic information via direct connection to Source. When the music flows, he is completely in an expanded state of consciousness, which allows the purest transmission of information to come forth. He is considered a master sound designer and creates all original sounds for his compositions, which is what gives his soundscapes their unique organic sound.

JoAnn Chambers/ShapeshifterTwo:
A Healer's Journey

JoAnn uses her clairvoyant/sentient/audient abilities to see energy patterns that emanate from thoughts, feelings and sounds. Symbols and images emerge that represent the energetic signature of the information that is being transmitted. She translates this information into several different forms of artistic expression in alignment with her kinesthetic attunement to multidimensional realms of guidance. As a graphic artist, she uses these talents to create all the art and graphics throughout Shapeshifter's projects. As a singer and sound healer, she also uses her voice in various ways to transmit higher teachings.

She is a psychophysical therapist and a vibrational healer. Her trainings and certifications include Postural Integration, massage LMT, cranialsacral therapy, neuromuscular therapy, esalan massage, reflexology, energy healing, yoga, movement and dance. She has maintained a private practice assisting others in awakening their creative potentials using many different techniques and modalities since 1985. She offers chakra readings, aura readings and pastlife readings as a way to explore one's current evolutionary cycles, as well as DNA Activation and Vibrational Healing sessions. She is currently available for remote sessions by request at The 3rd Eye (see back of guide).

The Creation Begins

Gary and JoAnn met several weeks after the Harmonic Convergence alignment in August of 1987. For those of you aware of this significant event, you will know that this was a powerful wake up call to many of the lightworkers and starseeds that were here in service to assist in the current planetary ascension process. This wave of energy swept across the planet and called many to align themselves with their soul purpose and mission work, which is exactly what had happened to Gary and JoAnn during their Harmonic Convergence celebrations. They both knew deep down that it was time for them to align with their spiritual soul mates on the earth plane and get on with what they came here to do. It was clear on many levels when they came together, that there was a deep pastlife connection and an agreement to reconnect in this lifetime to continue their work. They quickly realized that they had incarnated on earth-based planetary systems during key evolutionary cycles to bring through the Light-coded sonic frequencies in other significant timelines. Frequencies that are needed to assist in connecting the multidimensional realms of Light through harmonic resonance via sound/music.

As their work began, much information was released by working with the music that was being downloaded to them. These profound teachings of higher dimensional sound continues to be their guiding light to this day. These transmissions manifest and ground in alignment with the greater planetary timelines and activation cycles.

One of the first visions they became aware of when they recovered incarnational memories of their work together, was a special healing/transformational environment, they call The Odyssey. This was primarily from their Atlantean lifetime when crystal-based sound temples were used for healing and transformational work. The Odyssey contains a high end sound table, surround sound stereo system, sacred geometrics, energy enhancement items and many crystals. They created a sacred space and opened up a vortex that allowed for easier access to the higher realms, as well as safe passage to the Underworlds.

They soon realized that they had also previously been working towards the same energetic realizations in their individual work — that the DNA was actually the key to the communication and communion with the divine, the Source of ALL. These early realizations became the foundation for the expanded work they would bring to the planet through their male/female union and their commitment to grounding Light on the planet by assisting those ready to shift to the 5th dimensional light body. They would begin to build the frequency maps to this next level of existence.

In 1990, they were called to venture deep into the Amazon jungles to deepen their shamanic skills, awaken their dormant gifts and to test their levels of courage and strength for the road ahead. Years of teachings were compacted into this adventure that continues to influence their lives in many ways to this day. From studying with several indigenous shamans, experiencing native plant teachers and several life altering events, they emerged with an even deeper understanding of their work on the planet.

As they started to work together with clients, they developed a deep telepathic and empathic connection with each other which provided a safe space for clients to open up and release the blocked areas in their lives and to awaken their higher potentials. Gary's technology was plugged into the sound table in the Odyssey and he would play sounds and music specifically for the client in alignment with the healing work JoAnn was doing. This is how the DNA Activation soundscapes first began. In a sense, this was their research lab, observing the effects by watching the progression of their clients as well as their own. Personal music was composed for many clients during these sessions which the client worked with to further unfold the multi-level downloads of information received.

The energy vortex of The Odyssey created powerful shifts for both the client and for them. When JoAnn would enter areas of darkness/density/blockages within the clients auric layers, Gary would take them in with the music and let the sounds and frequencies establish a resonance with the energy and then lift the vibrational essence into the expanse of Light. They were both being shown how to communicate with the DNA from the energetic level of pure vibration.

The current LevelOne series of DNA music was birthed from these sessions which they did for 10 years (1989-1999). They continually evolve in their understanding and awareness of this work. Vibration, sound, frequency and music are the basis of the energetic dance of All That Is. It is their life's work to explore these realms on the leading edge of the awakening consciousness waves and to share these teachings with those who are ready to hear and willing to let go into the feeling and the bliss of the flow of life in the Harmonic Universe.

The sound design phase took over a year for Gary to develop a palate of sounds that he felt would represent the foundation for the DNA Activation process. He spent many hours in deep meditation tweaking each sound to get the right pitch, amplitude and modulation. It would be similar to seeing an artist creating a palate of paint colors prior to beginning the painting. Once the actual soundscapes came through, it was done in real time, using only 2 sound sources/synths at any given time. No overdubs/layers were added after the transmissions were received. Shapeshifter worked with individuals for many years to research/observe the results and effects that these soundscapes would have in peoples lives. The effects are varied depending on the individual focus, depth of commitment to their path, and their intent. Everyone who engaged deeply had positive results in all areas of their life and were clearly accelerating their evolutionary path.

The nascent work in sound healing and the effects of sound on the body human and consciousness were only just beginning to re-emerge within the human potential movement (early 90s). It was decided to keep the work contained to their private practice until such a time when more awareness about the profound nature of sound/vibration would begin to surface in the collective consciousness. As information and workshops started to come forth across the planet towards the later part of the 90s, the decision was made to make the music available to the people who were ready to receive these transmissions. The necessary bridges of information and techniques, which would eventually lead to the understanding of the power that sound/music/frequency will have on this unfolding process were being built by many of the great sound healing teachers. Each teacher brings through various aspects of the work so that the whole can be understood by those who choose to engage more deeply into the sound healing fields of study. Beyond the healing aspect, the next step is to understand this music as a transformational tool. A tool that will assist mankind in evolving to the next step on the evolutionary ladder of Light.

The next step following another level of equipment/technology upgrades, was the process of transferring these early transmissions into the higher quality digital recording format. Shapeshifter needed once again, to increase their technological understandings regarding the process of remastering the original recordings in to the digital domain, enhancing the sound quality to bring through the multi-dimensional aspects of the music even more.

Their initial research work with the LevelOne series finished around 1998 while living in the St. Pete, Florida area. They were called to move to a powerful Light center spot in the Western North Carolina mountains, Asheville. They spent the first 6 years semi-hibernating in a cabin in the woods, communing with nature and deepening their work. Using the internet as a way to reach out to the planet, they started releasing their soundscapes in January of 2000.

Shapeshifter has received guidance regarding this DNA series stating that there may be many levels that will come forth in their lifetime. Each successive series will come forth when certain energetic alignments have been made between the bio-energetic matrix of Shapeshifter, the collective signature of those beings who seek to integrate these frequencies and the planetary matrix.

DNA 1.5 Lucidity was released in 2011 during the time between these levels to support the transition - it is a bridge between the 2 levels. It was created to increase lucid states both in dreaming and awake states.

The DNA L2 soundscapes started to come forth in June 2008. This series is now available for those who have worked with the LevelOne series and have already integrated those frequencies. DNA L2 will be an accelerated program and available to those who are sincerely walking a dedicated path of Light and need the energetic sustenance to ground their various projects and works on the planet. More info in the back of this guide.

Use this space for notes, thoughts, ideas and experiences

Pre-Activation/Recapitulation Journal

As you begin your explorations with these DNA Activation soundscapes, you may want to spend some quiet, focused time to examine where you feel you are on your path. Make some notes about the current manifestation of your health, your personal life, your career, your manifestations and your abilities to hold higher frequencies of Light. The following questions can be used as a launching pad to stimulate thoughts, ideas and concepts to help you with this process. Use them to generate more thoughts on your own, as many more questions will come to you as you begin this process. We have provided several pages to record your insights. From time to time, you might want to return to these pages and review your entries, add some updates so that you can monitor your progress. As you move to each successive CD, we recommend that you take some time to record your journeys and make notes on the effects and benefits you are experiencing. In this way, you may begin to see patterns and relationships emerge. Review Listening Suggestion #26 - Recapitulatio for more information on using this technique to clear negative energy and increase your Light Quotient.

Physical Health

Examine the state of your overall health and well-being and make notes on any symptoms or problem areas that you may be having. List any chronic or acute complaints that you have been having in order of degree of severity. Make notes regarding the types of OTC or prescribed medications you may be taking now, as well as any alternative herbs, supplements, vitamins, vibrational essences, etc. that you may be ingesting as part of your health program. List any alternative therapies or treatments that you may be going through now and the results you are experiencing. Think about what areas of your physical body's health that you would like to have change or shift as a result of incorporating DNA Activation processes into programs to enhance your wellbeing. Examine your stress level and note how often you are in an agitated state and how often you are in a relaxed state.

Mental Health

Give thought to the current state of mental stability in your life. What types of thoughts do you focus on the most during your day? Do you consider yourself to have healthy, productive, positive thoughts or do you feel that you entertain thoughts that do not support your highest goals and aspirations? Make note on any common thoughts you have that seem to be repeating patterns in your life. Do you spend more time in your intellect and your imagination than in action and activities in your real world — Do you feel balanced in this regard? Do you have difficulty quieting your mind because you are so mentally active? Has your mental world overshadowed your emotional, feeling nature and how does this affect your reality?

Emotional Health

Examine your state of being and explore all your different emotional expressions. Be honest with yourself and write down which emotional states you spend most of you time in. Equate these emotional states with people, places or events in your life. What are your predominant emotional expressions? What feelings would you like to experience more of and which would you like to transform? Do you often feel that you need to defend your ideas, beliefs, viewpoints and experiences of life from attack from others with a more narrow perspective of reality? Have you ever considered that these defenses may relate to your childhood or pastlife experiences? How much do you hide your real self from your family, significant others and the world around you? How much fear and guilt do you hold about the life you live now and the life you would like to live? How do these feelings prevent you from living your full potential? How deeply do you allow yourself to experience the higher emotions of Love, Joy and Bliss? How open are you to expressing these feelings with others in your life?

Habits/Patterns/Addictions

List the habits/patterns/addictions in your life that you consider to be contributing to a lower vibrational experience of reality. Which of these do you want to change? What would you like to be doing and experiencing to move towards a more positive expansive reality? How open are you to change? Do you feel like you are stuck in a rut or groove that you can't seem to break free of? Have you considered that it might take some time for the new beliefs to take hold and are you willing to persevere long enough for this transition to actualize? What are you willing to start letting go of today in order to bring more Light into your life? Are you forcing change or are you learning to love and accept yourself as you are now, as an evolving being of Light who is growing and learning each day?

Career

Are you currently in a job or career path that brings you joy? If not, what is it about the job that is not fulfilling to you? What type of job or work would you prefer to be doing? If you did not have to work for financial needs, how would you spend your time.? What would your days be like if you could only do what you wanted to do with your time? How well are you utilizing your gifts and talents in your current position? How could things change within the current situation you are in now? What skills or talents do you need to bring forth in order to be doing something that would bring you more joy? Do you feel you have a mission in life or a reason that you are here and are you day by day taking the steps to actualize that vision? Do you believe in yourself enough to continuously work towards your highest goals and visions, even through the challenges that may appear in your life from time to time? What is your dream, your ideal source of abundance in exchange for your energy?

Family

Are you blessed with loving supportive family members that encourage you to follow your heart and to listen to your inner guidance? How does their presence in your life assist you in fulfilling your higher goals and aspirations? Do you feel nurtured and accepted for who you are? How do you react to the influence of their belief systems, cultural, religious, moral judgments, expectations, etc.? In your process of evolution, do you need to increase or decrease time with anyone in your family in order to remain in higher states of consciousness? How do you believe that you can transcend this perceived limitation? How can you raise the quality of your relationships to a Higher place of Love?

Social

Do you hold on to past out-moded relationships or do you surround yourself with friends who Love and support your higher dreams and visions? Are they supportive when you make changes and explore new, unknown areas or do they seem to attempt to manipulate your energy by holding you back to a place where they feel comfortable? Do you feel understood and listened to by your closest friends or those you come in to contact with? In conversations, do you attempt to dominate the energy or are you able to listen to others feelings and points of view? Is there jealousy and envy involved in your interactions? Do you feel unappreciated and not understood by the world at large? If you are searching for a mate or significant other, are you looking for Love in all the wrong places? Do you seek out places, events or groups that you feel resonance to in order to find a place where you can truly express your Light?

Spiritual Goals

This is the area where you should spend considerable time after you have reviewed the patterns of your life. Continue to go deeper into the music, asking for your highest purpose to be clearly shown to you through a loving connection to your Heart center, your Higher Self and The Source of All That Is. Keep exploring the many possibilities that emerge as you awaken and activate your multi-strand DNA matrix. What do you want to achieve this lifetime in relation to your spiritual progress? What lessons did you come here to complete? What karmic threads or patterns are you experiencing this lifetime that you still need to work through? Your life is a wondrous artistic expression born out of the choices you make each and every day, choose wisely and choose well. The choices you make today shape the future you experience tomorrow.

If you feel that you need additional support and guidance as you continue to walk this path, we are available to you in many ways. Please feel free to call us at 727.235.6302 during afternoon and early evening hours (EST zone). JoAnn, using her spiritual name, Shivanti is available for creative evolutionary guidance in the forms of DNA Activation Sessions, pastlife readings, aura portraits, chakra reading/balancing sessions, intuitive guidance and remote vibrational healing sessions in The Odyssey. You can request any of these readings at http://www.3rdEyeGuidance.com (more info at back of guide)

DISCLAIMER: (for obvious reasons) The information offered in this book should be considered spiritual in nature and not based in scientific fact. This type of guidance is not recognized to be truth by current medical or scientific models and should not replace your doctor's or other health care professional's opinions. You are ultimately responsible for the reality you experience and therefore create. This work is to be considered experimental and for adventurous explorers of consciousness.

SHAPESHIFTER DNA.L2 2012

Acceleration Frequencies for Lightworkers in Service
during the 2012-2023 alignment timelines

For updated info on this project VisionaryMusic.com/DNAL2-2012.html

The next level of this work emerged from a group of dedicated lightworkers that came together with a greater understanding of the importance behind this creation. This awareness truly goes beyond words and is something that is just known deep within at a soul level. As we unified with some common visions of what the possibilities and potentials were as we took this next step in humanity's evolution, we brought forth these new soundscapes into tangible manifestation. These soundscapes were rolled out in initiatory waves in alignment with the planetary ascension journey. We each had to integrate these sonic teachings at each step along the way. Then rolling that back into the next soundscape and so on until the project was completed in late 2011. The final 6 soundscapes were released beginning in January 2012 and carry a very wide spectrum of frequencies to guide you through the 2012-2023 timelines, aligning you more fully with your path, purpose and higher mission work on the planet.

This is another step into our Sonic Mystery School, one that has no rules, no dogmas or guidelines that you must follow - nothing to join. You only need to extend yourself out into the multidimensional realms of Light and ask for the guidance you need to fully actualize your purpose and accomplish your mission parameters. The music acts as your guide on this journey, accessing portals and gateways as you need, leading you towards the connections you need that manifest as synchronicity.

Once you have spent around 6 months with the LevelOne series, you should consider moving on to this DNA.L2 series. LevelOne is your foundation, this series is for when you are really ready to fully step up and walk your path of Light above all else.

Conscious Evolution through Multidimensional Music & Sound

Support your Evolutionary Path of Light

DNA.LevelOne.Activation.1 2 3 4 — From the deepest space within, waveforms of a higher implicate order resonate the codes within the DNA, unfolding the magic and wonder of all that you truly are. This set is a powerful channeling of original soundscapes created with the intent to activate the codex within the DNA, the bridge between the multiple dimensions of matter and the Divine. Travel on cyber-shamanic journeys into the many faceted realms of Light and Awareness. Each CD is a 50 minute journey shapeshifting through the infinite probable realities of your being, awakening and activating your unfolding potential. The soundscapes of this series are very multidimensional, shifting and changing each time you listen. Utilized with conscious intent, they are profoundly powerful tools to prepare you for the next wave in evolution now manifesting on the planet.

DNA Activation Book - This book contains comprehensive information regarding Shapeshifter's approach to DNA Activation through music/sound as well as answers to many frequently asked questions regarding this work.

See also **AYD Training Program** (page 84)

DNA 1.5 Lucidity
DNA 1.5 is a bridge, an encoded gateway of sonic transmissions that will take you from the foundations of DNA Activation LevelOne into the more expansive shamanic multidimensional worlds of DNA.L2.2012. As the inertial pull of the 3D world spirals downward into a generated control structure illusion of darkness and fear, limitation and lack; the new 5th World of Light rises up in a necessary response with a clearer expression of our divine heritage.

Shamballa~Journey Home — There is a place within all of us that is collectively known as Home. As ancient legends and myths throughout history have foretold, this sacred space may be experienced as a manifestation in 3D or as an inner sanctuary of multidimensional experience. In truth All is One. Within our DNA, lies the mystery and magic of Shamballa, simply waiting for you to initiate the process of awakening. As each soul travels their own path on the Journey Home, we continually raise our Light Quotient as we move into alignment with the waves of energy from the Galactic Core, through the Living Sun. The first CD in this on-going series provides you with profound frequency maps to harmonize your body temple and its surrounding energetic fields with this vast influx of loving energy. This soundscape is a tangible manifestation, a gift in response to our collective calling, that you can utilize in your daily life to initiate and actualize your experience of Heaven on Earth.

The Odyssey — Designed for explorations in Shapeshifter's original surround sound vortex, The Odyssey™, these sonic landscapes will ground your energy, balance your chakras and harmonize your auric field. The deep bass tones create a continuous subtle vibrational effect on the physical body which allows the undulating modulations and melodies to stretch and expand the etheric energy bodies. The music cycles through various themes, as various spiraling, swirling and rhythmic sounds engage the listener. The intent behind this music is to create a unified field within and around the human bio-energetic matrix, in preparation for altered states of exploration, shamanic journeys, out of body experiences and other ascension dynamics.

Healing — Warm and vibrant electronic keyboard melodies that gently invite the listener to travel on an inward journey to connect with their soul in blissful communion. Tones, sounds, patterns and pulses that will awaken dormant memories of past lives and ancient wisdom lying deep within the cellular structure of the body. A gentle celebration of life; a timeless composition that can be used throughout ones lifetime in many ways — from pre-birth to final transition. The melodies in this higher vibrational music were created with the intent of creating wholeness, uplifting the vibrational essence and returning one's conscious awareness to The Source.

Myth, Magic & Mystery — 8 shamanic journeys that invite you to travel deep into inner realms of imagination and creativity. Excellent for visualization and developing clairvoyant abilities. Recommended for driving, creative playtime, dancing/movement & work environments as well as creative meditation work. Babies & children also love this CD as it contains a variety of unusual and evocative sounds that stimulate the creative spark.

*A portion of all monies received will support the development of EVO, a non-profit foundation for supporting higher creativity and conscious evolution through music & multimedia technology.

DNA Activation/Shapeshifter

Abundance Series: Sanctuary

This music will connect you through a Rainbow Bridge with the profound assistance now available from the Shining Ones - the Elementals, Devics, Sidhe, Fae, Leprechan and Elven realms. This communion will transform your reality in a new, different, more profound and multi-faceted way than you have ever experienced. These vast and wise energies are actively and energetically participating with us in the creation of this music through the gifting of these harmonic and melodic invocations. Allowing oneself to deeply commune with these energies through these sonic gateways will bring the empowering essence of that magic into the greatest life affirming tangible transformation, abundance and manifestation into all aspects of your lives.

Transmissions of Light Codes Series

All soundscapes in this series emanate from our live concert performances. The music and vocal chanting are recorded and later mixed into a final album. Each concert begins with a focused intention and all performers and participants hold focus on this throughout the event bringing together a unifying group experience in alignment with the higher dimensions of Light. These tramsmissions of light codes are received in the purest states of Love, Compassion, Abundance and Unity for all sentient beings on the Planet.

Journey towards Abundance

As one evolves on their spiritual journey, the subject of Ascension is one that comes up to awaken them to the next step in their evolving adventure into the many realms of Light. This transmission begins with the step towards engaging more deeply with the concepts of Ascension. This soundscape is a very soft and gentle flowing piece that is ideal for all types of healing work, massage, energy and reiki sessions. Can be listened to as background music in therapeutic offices and excellent for sleep time.

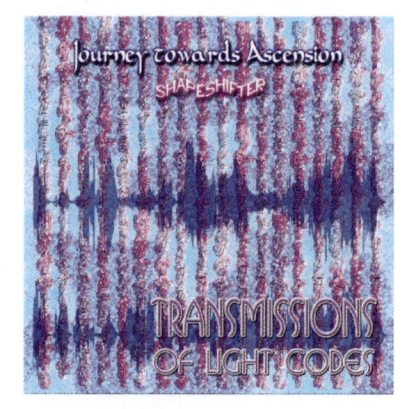

Aya's Underworld

The Underworld is filled with lost power and strength which can be used to walk deeper into your spiritual path of becoming. This soundscape is has a lot of energy, movement and powerful shamanic rhythms, taking you deeper and deeper into the Underworlds. Contains some deep shamanic chanting to assist in the Underworld adventure. There are many dark passages to assist you in delving into your subconscious realms where lost power and energy will be found.

5TH WORLD EMERGING

The world as it has been known to be is primarily a 3rd dimensional reality construct, which we call 3D. As humanity is now evolving and raising their Light Quotient to the next higher realms of manifestation, we emerge into the 5th Dimensional realms. It is in this 5D realm that one can begin to understand/comprehend how we exist in a multidimensional reality, by viewing their existence from a higher perspective than was previously thought possible. This is the realm that has been called Heaven on Earth or the 5th World template/matrix. Let yourself become the architect of this new world, building the necessary structures and templates that will allow you to hold your primary focus in 5D which still manifesting tangible forms in 3D.

Check our website and submit your email address to keep up with our latest releases.

ReJuva, the first CD in our Abundance series, begins with the primal energy of Water, a catalyst and a conductor of Light and Lifeforce. It is a precursor, a transporter of energy and information necessary for transformation and rejuvenation of the Body Temple (composed of almost 70% water). It is also a major factor in the activation and initiation of the multi-strand DNA codex. The intent within the ReJuva soundscape is to assist in restructuring water's essence into the most open and fluid matrix of potentials and possibilities. The primary purpose behind the creation of ReJuva is to awaken awareness of the living intelligence and wisdom of the Body Temple's crystalline water structure. Through empathic resonance of this awareness and awakening knowledge, energetic evolutionary signals are transmitted to the cellular matrix, greatly enhancing the biophotonic flow in the process of DNA to RNA transport. With openness, receptivity and conscious engagement the physical being of the experiencer becomes increasingly more conductive and receptive to a higher vibrational matrix of manifestation and personal empowerment. If you engage deeply with this music, you will find it to be one of the most powerful tools on the planet for assisting in the emergence of the LightBody; in alignment with the unfolding ascension process. If done with heartfelt sincerity, resonance and participation, you will initiate the next stage of multidimensional abundance, experience and awareness. Through the clarity of sound and intent, which builds up with each successive track, there is an adding, blending and balancing of the other four archetypal elemental keys — Earth, Fire, Air and Spirit/Aether — into the evolving mix. Riding upon and within these sonic transmissions of empowerment is the energetic of the next level of Abundance. As one balances, integrates, opens and raises their vibration to a more expansive perception of manifestation, one also receives more and more support from the Universe and from Gaia. This establishes a direct connection to the next ascendent level of wellbeing, wealth, happiness and a joyous sense of purpose.

ABUNDANCE SERIES

The Secret of Abundance: ReJuva (Book)

The book will expand upon the teachings in the ReJuva soundscape, so they are meant to be worked with together. It will help you to apply higher principles to the work you are doing with the music. Abundance is our birthright and one that can be applied to your life once you understand some of the basic principles. In order to consistently engage with the energetic constructs that attract Abundance into your life, you will need to raise the vibration of your body temple and all the interactions you are engaged with.

The material in the guide will cover many teachings and principles to explore when seeking rejuvenation of the body temple in order to hold the higher frequencies and manifestation of Abundance on all levels. The guide is a magical talisman that unfolds more secrets of higher level transformation the more you engage with the process.

Take our Webinar titled: Embracing Abundance: Making Money as Lightworker
(available under Webinars Link on our Home Page)

ReJuva Healing Wand Pendant

These beautiful and powerful healing wand pendants are an excellent tool to work with while rejuvenating the Body Temple with ReJuva and can be worn as a necklace to charge your water and all foods/drinks before entering the body. They can also be used as a pendulum to determine the compatibility of the substances you ingest. Each piece will be specifically attuned to your energy by Shapeshifter using the Odyssey EEE and Grandfather Crystal to personalize and empower each piece. It is an excellent tool to use during meditation work by placing on any of your chakras. These wands are wrapped with sterling silver. The wand is a 12 sided natural quartz crystal Vogel cut wand approximately 1-1/2" long and the entire pendant is approximately 2-1/4". The ametrine is octagonal (emerald cut). The garnet is a trillion cut (triangle-brilliant). There are 2 small AAA fine herkimer diamonds.

DNA Activation/Shapeshifter

AYD (Activate Your DNA) Training Program

Shamanic Journeys into the Multidimensional Timestream

AYD #1 & #2

http://www.visionarymusic.com/Workshops/AYD/AYD1.html

To enhance your knowledge and attain deeper experiences with the soundscapes, we highly recommend that you begin to expand your awareness and understanding by working with this training series. Each module will build on the preceding one, initially building the foundation and then taking you deeper into working with sound to transform your realities and perceptions of what it is to become a multidimensional being of Light. Each module features an opening narration, animation of the teaching, audio vocal tracks, music and guided journeys.

AYD #1 Building a Solid Spiritual Foundation
(grounding, balancing chakras, increasing Light, connecting with Higher Self, Activating your DNA)

AYD #2 Working with Multidimensional Sound
(developing point of focus and expanding field of awareness via color and sound, modulating energy, shapeshifting and energy body development)

Available on DVD or as individual downloads

Evolutionary Guidance for those who Walk the Spiritual Path of Light

All of our readings and healing sessions support the work you are doing with the Shapeshifter soundscapes. Personal transformation requires the examination of many belief systems. The core of our shared existence is at the threshold of change and shifts are occurring rapidly. This transition will illuminate the way we interact with ourselves, family, friends and our environment as we move into a new, more expansive way of being. JoAnn Chambers/Shivanti is available for the following sessions, which can assist you in working with the multidimensional soundscapes and assist you in holding focus on your path and unfolding your divine purpose for incarnating at this time. Sessions are done remotely, via email, live chat or phone. Shivanti has maintained a private practice since 1985 beginning with massage/bodywork/psychophysical therapy and gradually evolved into an internet based practice working remotely with clients all over the world. She is a clairvoyant shaman who can see into many dimensional realms to assist clients in discovering their deeper truths on their healing journey.

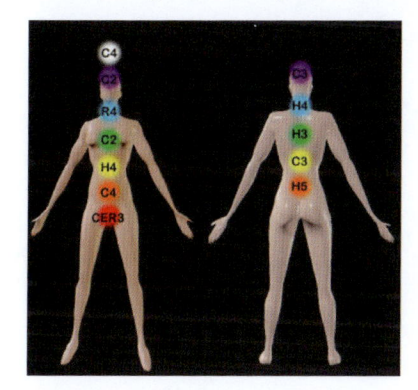

Chakra Portrait/Reading & Balancing Session - using a 12 chakra system to read the status of the chakra energy system, a portrait is offered to help you understand where you are at this time on your evolutionary path. This is followed by a 24 hour remote healing session in the Odyssey Sound & Light Healing Room. This is an excellent way to monitor your spiritual progress.

Pastlife Readings - going deep into core level pastlife imprints that create patterns in one's life that are repeated until awareness and undestanding emerges is the focus of this type of reading. By learning how these threads of energy carry forth into our current lives, we can learn how to release, let go and forgive so we can move on with more strength as we release these hidden fears.

Aura Portrait/Reading - by clairvoyantly viewing all the layers of your auric field, a graphic image is created to see what energetics you are working and operating from. Guidance is offered to help you work with these imprints for clearing and empowering your unfolding process.

Spiritual Guidance - sometimes just sharing ideas and thoughts with a spiritual guide can help one to move through energy that might be stagnant or blocking one from moving along on the next step of the journey. These can be done via email, chat or phone.

DNA Activation Sessions - using the DNA Activation soundscapes, a 24 hour vibrational healing session is done in the Odyssey Sound and Light Healing Room to assist one in their activation process. Sessions can be done for each of the 4 soundscapes.

Vibrational Healing - a 24 hour remote healing session in the Odyssey Sound & Light Healing Room. The focus can be whatever it is you are wanting to work on at the time of the session.

PRIVATE SESSIONS ARE AVAILABLE IN FLORIDA in the Odyssey - CONTACT JOANN FOR MORE DETAILS

3rdEyeGuidance.com

awaken@3rdeyeguidance.com
828.301.7410

Listen to Shivanti's Teleconferences on Talkshoe Radio - see Home page (Podcasts available)

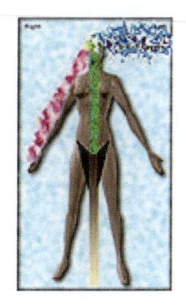

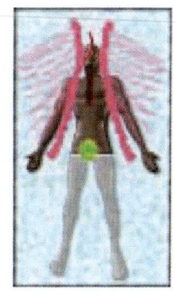

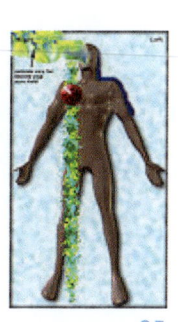

EVO
Center for Creative Evolution
(non-profit foundation - in process)

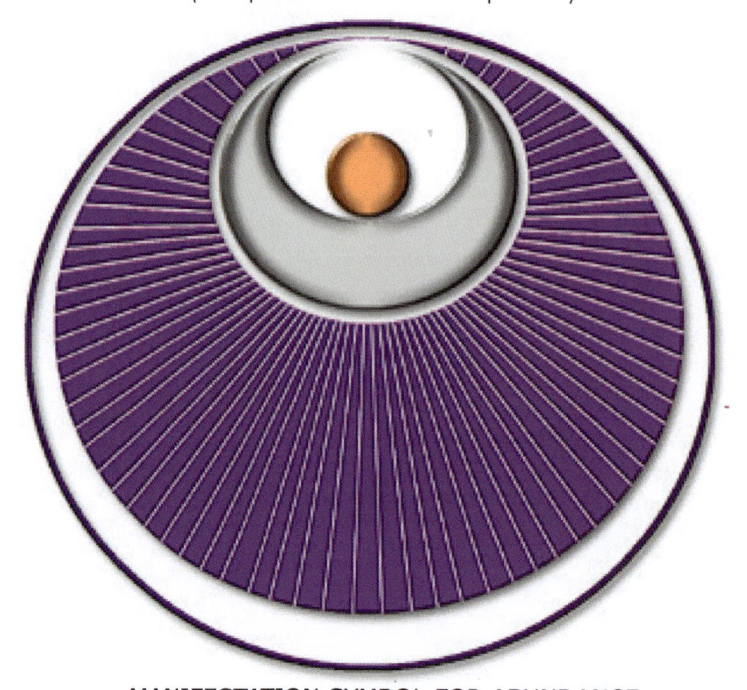

MANIFESTATION SYMBOL FOR ABUNDANCE

Our Financial Angel Logo was created based on a crop circle design that appeared in a field in July 2001. It has been called the Cambridge Angel. We chose this image to represent Financial Abundance, Freedom and Prosperity for ALL. Poster Prints & Desktop Pictures are available on-line.

EVO Foundation's Mission: To provide financial and technological support to the planet's most gifted creatives in actualizing their multimedia based projects. Their gifts begin the creation of an alternative and aware media network that will, in a profound and timely manner - uplift, transform, and inspire humanity.

Decide to support the manifestation of this mission and contribute to this fund. We welcome your donation in the spirit of abundance and prosperity for all who have been called to follow their hearts and the guidance they are receiving in order to ground the multidimensional realms of Light to our beautiful planet. The more resources, the more expansive the possibilities. Every calling that is honored, every window that is opened, every step that is taken, allows the manifestation of the most open and positive outcomes to occur. These donations are used to support the on-going mission and to eventually create this foundation to support those who follow.

More Information and updates on our progress: http://www.VisionaryMusic.com/EVO.html

Send your Donations to:
Visionary Music, Inc.
(request address or send via PayPal)
paypal@visionarymusic.com

SHAPESHIFTER

Events | Workshops | Concerts | Sound Healing Events

Check our calendar or MeetUp groups for our most current and up to date listings of events.

DNA Activation/Shapeshifter

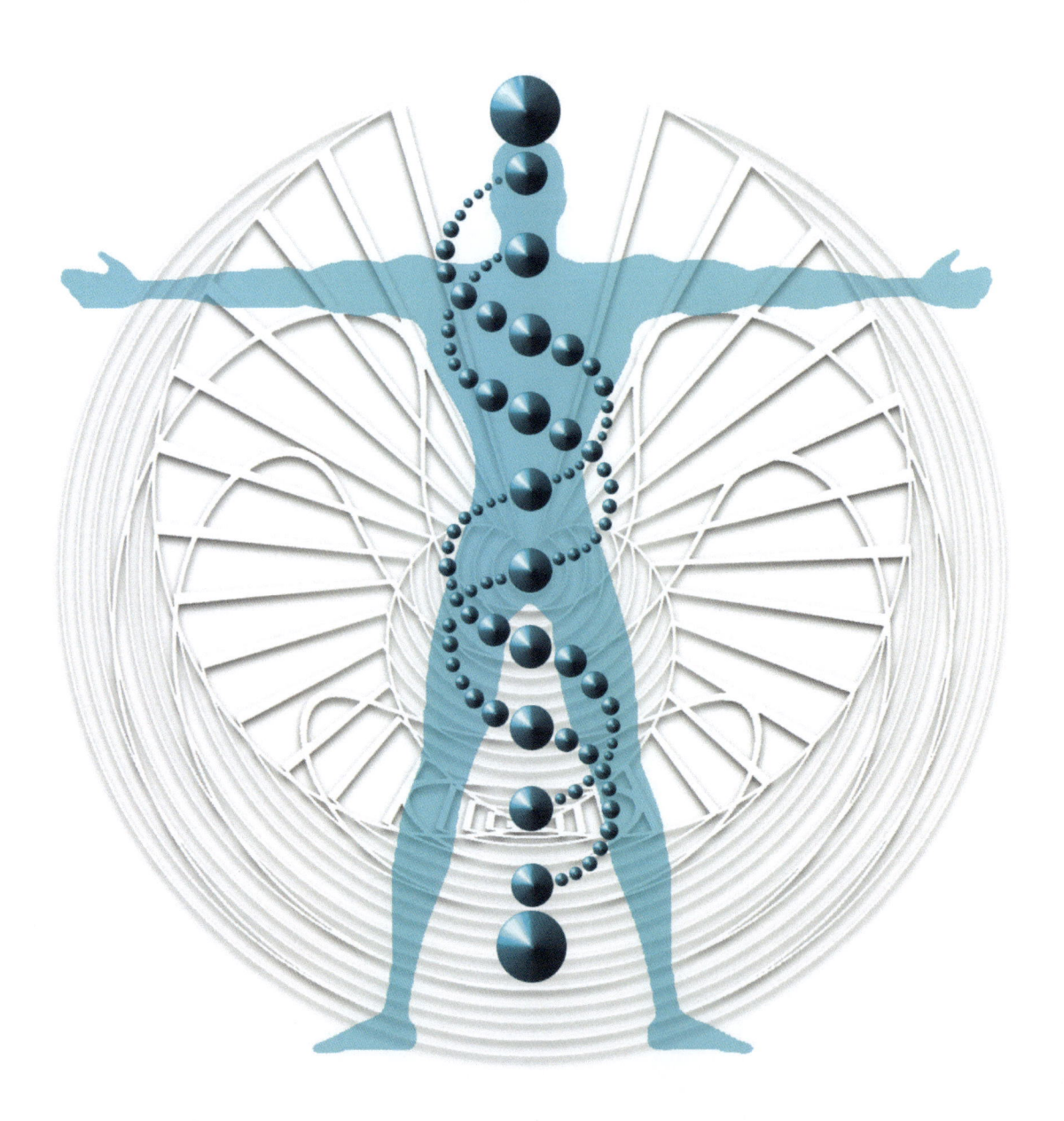

Printed in Great Britain
by Amazon